One of Those Women

Cynthia A. Williams

Edited By
Deborah McMullan
Charles A. Williams

© 2001 by Cynthia Williams

One of Those Women
by Cynthia Williams

Printed in the United States of America
ISBN 1-931232-63-6

All rights reserved. No part of this publication may be reproduced or transmitted in any form or by any means without written permission of the publisher.

Xulon Press
344 Maple Ave. West, #302
Vienna, VA 22180
703-691-7595
XulonPress.com

All rights reserved. This book is protected under the copyright laws of the United States of America. This book may not be copied or reprinted for commercial gain or profit. The use of short quotations or occasional page copying for personal or group study is permitted and encouraged. Permission will be granted upon request.

In his heart a man plans his course, but the Lord determines his steps.

Proverbs 16:9 (KJV)

This book is true. The names have been changed to protect the privacy of all those concerned.

satan and any reference made to him is not capitalized throughout the text. It is not a grammatical error. I give him no prominence.

TABLE OF CONTENTS

Dedications vii
Acknowledgements ix
Introduction. 1
Chapter One—Why Me? 3
Chapter Two—The Curse. 15
Chapter Three—Chosen 19
Chapter Four—Marriage of Convenience 23
Chapter Five—Married to a Backslider 41
Chapter Six—My Spiritual Wedding 57
Chapter Seven—Satan's Demonic Devices. 63
Chapter Eight—The Boulder. 85
Chapter Nine—Unconditional Forgiveness 99
Chapter Ten—The Test. 111
Chapter Eleven—Chosen Too. 115
Chapter Twelve—How You Like Me Now? 125
Chapter Thirteen—Set Your House In Order 137
Chapter Fourteen—Guard Your Heart. 145
Chapter Fifteen—The Ultimate Choice 151
Works Cited 159
About the Author 161

DEDICATIONS

I dedicate this book to My Lord and Savior Jesus Christ who delivered me from the curse, birthed this ministry in my spirit, and allowed me to see the light through all the darkness. I love you, Lord.

I dedicate this book to my mother who wailed, and cried out for her children. Mom, your prayers were answered. "Wailing Women Win." I love you Mom.

I dedicate this book to my children who continued to love me despite the toils and strife they endured while I was living this ministry. I love you.

I dedicate this book to my husband, my Adam, who God has so patiently set apart for me. I thank God for his forgiveness and the love God has placed in him for me. Will, I love you.

Last but not least, I dedicate this book to all the hurting individuals that are victims of generational curses. Receive the Word, "No Longer."

ACKNOWLEDGEMENTS

There are so many people whom I've never met personally, however we share the same spirit. I know God has truly blessed their lives because they have truly blessed mine.

I would like to thank God for the following people and their ministries that shed light in my spirit.

First, all the military men of God, Chaplains Jordan, Maney, Jones and Reed for allowing God to use them to feed my spirit.

Bishop T.D. Jakes, my spiritual daddy. Yes, the woman is loosed and celebrating with her lover and her Lord, the ministry and the songs truly graced my spirit with joy, unspeakable joy.

Bishop Paul Morton, I finally have life. Thank you for the Life Series.

Bishop Clarence McClendon, my husband is chosen and coming out of Egypt.

Pastor Rod Parsley for the revelation of the awesome breakthrough anointing, and allowing the anointing to flow through his millenium journal, and sharing in the same vision God has given me - the Resurrection Generation.

Pastor Ed Montgomery, Heaven truly is in my heart.

Kenneth and Gloria Copeland, I'm Abraham's daughter, Chosen of God.

Iyanla Vanzant for 40 days and 40 nights of spiritual and personal growth.

Rebecca Brown & Daniel Yoder for revealing the curses that had me bound, yet now I'm Free!!

Detrick Haddon, TriNiTi 57, Fred Hammond, Third World, and Lauryn Hill for their ministry of music that blessed my spirit with messages that ministered deep. A special blessing for CeCe Winans, this is the Oil that fills my Alabaster box, and he's finally ready.

I also acknowledge my neighbor, my sister, my friend, Patricia Smith, who was there for me and never said a mumbling word, I love you.

I would also like to thank all those that assisted me in the fight to get this book to publish, Deborah McMullan, Enrique Rivera, Eduardo Benavides, and so many others, be blessed for allowing God to allow you to bless me.

INTRODUCTION

I lived my life as most everyone does. I just did it, without much thought as to why I was doing what I was doing or who was ultimately in control. I got hurt many times, and I hurt others in many ways. I never meant to, it was just me, or who I thought I was.

I often felt there were forces at work in my life, but I never considered the magnitude of those forces. I finally understand what the Bible means when it says, there's a war between satan and God, which for many means knowing whether to go left or to go right, whether to follow the truth or believe a lie, ultimately whether to live or die.

It's really simple. There are two forces that rule this world, and God has given us the free will to make a choice which force we will allow to control our life. God allows us to make the moves in this game called life, however, there's always a catch. We have an opposing force. Yes, satan was kicked out of Heaven, and came here to keep us from making the right choice and that dilemma makes the choice a difficult one. Not that I don't want to live right, or make the right choices, it's just so hard when you're under constant attack, and satan really attacks those that are Chosen. So watch out! If your life is a mess, you're broken and being broken, know that, God has planted seeds in you, and satan wants to steal and destroy them. Don't allow it. Read the book and see just how devious satan can be in his journey to kill your seed. Then, watch God be God, victorious in every battle. Open your spirit to receive today. Enjoy.

CHAPTER ONE

WHY ME?

Nay but, O man, who art thou that repliest against God? Shall the thing formed say to Him that formed it, Why hast thou made me thus? Hath not the potter power over the clay, of the same lump to make one vessel unto to honour, and another unto dishonour?
Romans 9: 20,21 (KJV)

I sit here at the table, tears rolling down my eyes and in my mind, I ask the question, Why me? Why has life treated me with such disgust? Why do I always make the wrong decisions especially when they all seem so right. I look at my life, and it seems it was set for doom from the beginning. I sit here crying and even consider dying, but I look at all the good things that have become a part of my life, and I can't even seriously contemplate the thoughts that continue to whirl around in my head. Thoughts like, what would happen if I just end it now? I hate it. My life is not my own. It belongs to Christ, who is my Lord and Savior, but sometimes I have to ask the Lord, why me? Why must I continue to go through the heartache of what seems to be continuous mistakes.

I'm far from perfect. I acknowledge I need God's help, but where is the Lord when I make these bonehead decisions? Why doesn't He stop me? I hurt so many people, and I look so stupid. You would think I'd learn one day from all the mistakes I continue to make, but I keep on, and now it seems as if I've made the biggest mistake of all, and my world is coming tumbling down around me. I'm watching it slowly slip through my fingers. I don't know where to turn. I cry out to the Lord every moment, but He seems to leave me to get myself out of this mess.

Lord what am I to do? All of this brings me back to the very beginning. The very first things I can remember, and again it wasn't good. It's never been good. Again, I ask myself, Why Me?

I remember being only two years old, left alone in the cold with no one to love or care for me. Evidently, the one I loved most couldn't take care of me because they couldn't take care of themselves. Why does love have to hurt so bad when love is suppose to be the answer to God's quest and desire, why He created man anyway? However, in the name of love, my mother tried to kill me and my two sisters, then kill herself because she loved a man that didn't love her, or didn't seem to love her. Was it really love or was it some strange thing that happens to some people to make them lose all their senses and do the stupidest things they could possibly imagine. But, why me?

Why did I get left in the cold? Why not my sisters? Why, because my dad, or the only man I ever called dad, and the only man I knew as a dad, left me behind, to die in the cold of the winter snow, tied to a tree, only after the attempt my mother made to take our heads off with an ax failed. I thank God for a grandfather who loved me and took me in when my dad took my sisters to Missouri to his mother, and had my mother committed to an asylum.

She lost her mind. She was heartbroken and defeated, as I

too seem today. The only man she loved betrayed her and married another without getting a divorce or even allowing her the benefit of thinking he had fallen out of love with her. Hmm, bigamy, could this be something passed down through the generations? No closure, just questions. Doubt and deception, the devil's master tools. In a fit of rage and pain, she sought revenge and brought me into this world, along with another child who didn't survive the turmoil or the trip. She entered into eternal peace before the tribulation for her even began. She was stillborn. Oh lucky me, or should I say, lucky her. That one point in my life is a scar, a scar I will never forget. It will always aggravate me. I thought I was over it, but every time I look at my life, that's the first picture I see.

A woman in rage, from hurt and pain, all in the name of love, tying her three children to a tree in the backyard, in the dead of winter, in the snow and taking an ax to their heads, like turkeys at Thanksgiving. My soul says thank you for my grandfather who grabbed the ax and stopped what could have been three vicious murders and a suicide. Sometimes I wish he'd been too late. It would all be over. That is life, as I've known it, would never have happened.

God, it's been so hard. Every turn has been another drama to add to the last one. What a beginning. Is this truly what one calls life? I don't know, but sometimes I just want to get off the wheel. I just want to quit, but I can't see myself doing what my mother attempted to do. I guess we play to the tune of a different drummer because at this point in my life, I have something my mother didn't have. I have Christ. My mother didn't meet Him until after she tried the only thing she felt she could do to end the drama and be at peace, even if that peace meant eternal damnation and torment.

The cost of ignorance, but thank God for being God because He came into my mother's life when she was in the hospital.

She surrendered to the Truth, and gave her life to Christ. That was the beginning of her life. A life full of trials and tribulations which everyone in Christ will encounter, but sometimes it seems some of us just have to encounter so much more than others. Why? Why me?

The memories continue to linger, but only the ones that seem to devastate my life stick in my mind. I remember the reason why my dad left me behind when my mother tried to kill us. I was five years old, and I was doing what any normal child does. I was being nosey. I was looking through my dad's bureau drawers, when he hit me. My dad wasn't known for hitting us, but he slapped me. Right then, he said, I wasn't his child. Yes, that's what came out his mouth. "You're not my child, anyway." That statement has been deeply embedded in my mind since then.

I guess that's how and why most of my life is the way it is. You see, unaware or unconsciously, I spent all my young life trying to prove to my dad, that man, I was worthy of his love. Consequently, that's also what I've spent all my adult life doing, trying to prove to men I'm worthy of their love, when they really aren't worthy of mine. They say sticks and stones will break your bones, and words will never hurt you. That's a lie. Whoever made up that line, know they lied because words are the eternal knife that cut the soul. It hurts every time I think of him saying, I wasn't his child. I think of how he abandoned me when my mother tried to kill us. It hurts. Physically hurts. My gut wretches in pain, and I want to cry. I loved that man, and I did all I could to make myself worthy of his love.

I was always considered the smartest in the family. I don't think it was really true. I think it's only because I tried the hardest. I did everything for him. I got good grades, read and wrote poetry, played all the sports and excelled in all of them. Despite being fat and dumpy, I was always first string in basketball, softball, field hockey, and track. I even worked for that man. I was his slave labor when he had his lawn business. I hired the neighborhood kids for minimal wages. We all worked for one fourth of what he was getting paid, but he wasn't doing any of the work. I stayed around my dad and learned whatever he was willing to teach me, which wasn't good, since my dad was a hustler and loan shark. He was the biggest thief I knew, even though, he did it with class. He peddled food stamps. People on welfare would rather have money instead of food stamps, and he was all too willing to oblige.

My dad was the black Nixon on the Beach, and quite the ladies man, old women and young women alike. He did my mother so wrong, but she stuck by him, despite the fact. She was doing what God called a wife to do, even though her heart was breaking every day. We, her children, had to watch her pain, and the turmoil that resulted in our lives. They say children live what they learn, but what we learned was not all that, in fact, it was not that at all. We learned to steal, to lie, and to be promiscuous. Then, we would be called sluts, whores, Jezebel's, and any other name a female having sex can be called by a man, and this man just happened to be my dad. The same man that taught us all we knew, by running around with all the tramp women he could find, and every once in a while, he'd have a class act.

I just went a drift, but looking back into my life, I can't help it. It's really hard to put on paper. The drama was just that, drama, constantly! You know, I mention the people that probably influenced my life the most. First, my mother. When I think of her, tears come to my eyes because my mother was my heart. She was my world. When she left, or when God chose to take her, a big big part of me left with her. For a long time, I blamed God for taking my mother. She was the only one I had in this life. No one else loved or cared for me. She protected me from that man, I called my dad. Despite what I did, he always treated me differently. He didn't buy me any school clothes, or schoolbooks. He never went to any of my events. He just never seemed to care, but my mom was always there for me. She ensured all my needs were met. I guess she was kind of my God, which is what a mom is supposed to be. That's a mother's ministry.

My mother was really more than that. She was the epitome of what a mother is suppose to be. It was as if, after her breakdown, she was determined to be all God called her to be in a mother's ministry. She was also the wife, whenever my dad decided he would be at home and not with another woman. All the children loved my mother, even my enemies loved my mother, and she loved them, despite how I felt about them. She was the neighborhood mother. She took care of and educated all the children, not just her own. She was the liaison, the counselor, the mediator, the confidant, and the taxi.

My mother was dying. She knew she was dying, as her own mother had died a young death. She educated me, and all the children she encountered on life, and all it's ups and downs. Her premature death was traumatic, in all the stages it took, in that my mother did things only God Himself could understand. Those things many people used to label her as being 'crazy,' to include her own daughter. I knew my mother wasn't crazy. She was definitely connected. God said we are a peculiar people, therefore, we do peculiar things, and she did, but she never hurt anyone. She loved and helped everyone, right up to her very death. She didn't spend her time trying to teach me how to cook or do the so-called woman things. She knew I would eventually have to learn. She taught me about life, and all it entailed. Only she couldn't teach me about men because she had never encountered more than two, and the one she really loved, betrayed her, was disloyal and unfaithful until death did them part. He broke her heart. Ultimately, I would go so far as to say she didn't die of man's diagnosis, lung cancer. She died of a broken heart, a crushed spirit. It was evident at her death, as her eyes locked on my dad, as he sat at her beside.

That was my mom, the salt of the earth. Then, there was my dad. Mister Casanova, the ladies man, Mister Gigilo and all that. He had a woman at every port. He made sure of it. He spent twenty-two years of his twenty-four year military career out to sea. From port to port, seeing his women, and collecting his portfolio. Yes, he brought home pictures, and kept photo albums. What a man. A married man who made a baby every time he dropped in town. You know that old saying, "Keep em bare foot and pregnant." Well, that's what he tried to do, and for the time he spent at home, that's exactly what he did. The only good thing I can say about this man I call daddy is, he provided for our family. Unlike any of the men I tend to encounter. I guess my dad taught his daughters all to well how to be self sufficient and independent, how not to need a man like him or any other kind. God, I want to ask if that was good or bad. Sure, I can take care of myself, but I can't seem to find a man to take care of me, or want to. Not that I need him too, but it is what God charged a man to do. Yes, to take care of his queen, his virtuous woman. Help me Lord.

I look at my life, and I see nothing but mistakes and turmoil, one after another. I want to cry because it seems so hopeless. Yet, I can't seem to let go. I can't throw in the towel because of all that God has put in me. I want so much more for me and my children, but I can't seem to get out of this stream of destruction. Life seems such a waste. It seems as though destiny is just a trip in the Egyptian wilderness without Moses to help me cross the Red Sea. Sometimes I wish I had never met Jesus. I wish He had not allowed me to go through all I've been through, which lets me know He is God, and He is in control. He is a rewarder of those that diligently seek Him. He will make a way out of no way. The stories I can tell you about Him would rock your world. Stories, testimonies now, I had no idea He was even a part of until I look back now and see He has always kept me from being my own worst enemy.

All during high school, during my times of drugs and sexual encounters, I realize now God was there with me and for me. He was the keeper of my soul even before I knew Him as I do now. He knows the plans He has for me, plans to prosper and not to harm me, but to bring me to an expected end. God knows I should be riddled with AIDS, and every other sexually transmitted disease, even though, I thank Him I never had any. I say this because I took the dreaded family curse of promiscuity, and I had my toil in it. I know every man I encountered sexually. The numbers are more than any decent female could ever claim to even mention in a secret conversation. I kept every name and detail. I even ranked each by there endowedness and their skill at what they thought was something special, but to me was just a fulfillment of a curse. A curse I was plagued with because of my dad. The world defines such behavior as dysfunctional. Lie. The Bible, the Truth, calls it a generational curse. A curse that had to be broken. But out of all of them, all the men, there was never any love. That ugly and disgusting word "Love." The ultimate goal of life, " Love." I wish I could encounter even the simplest form and live to see that it really does exist, and see that God's love can present itself in man. I really would like to see that we all aren't just caught up in fleshly desires.

I continue to ask, why me? I want to do what's right, but it always seems to turn out wrong. I never want to hurt anyone, least of all myself, but I keep doing just that. I ask myself, why do I do the things I do? I know it's never out of a selfish and devilish heart, but the outcome is still the same, and it seems so sinister. I want to do good for everyone, but most of all, I want to do God's will which doesn't always seem to be what I thought it was or is. I cry at night, and pray to God, but the answers I get only seem to hurt the ones I say I love because deep in my heart, I do love them. I love them deeply and dearly.

Everyone keeps saying you ought to write a book about all your life encounters, but some seem so unbelievable it's really hard for me to put on paper. Sometimes, I think I'm crazy because the things that happen to me don't happen to normal people, but what's normal? I see God in everything I do, and everything that happens. I hear people say I make God fit whatever I do, but I know that it's only their carnal eyes they're looking through and not the eyes of God because God did say trust Him and acknowledge Him in all your ways. These things seem so peculiar and strange, only a child of God could believe they are real. It seems so hard to live and do God's will in this life. Life where satan has been given free reign, and everyone is focused on everything except Christ.

I look at the Book, the Bible, the foundation, and I realize everyone should rely on His Word, but they can't seem to see past the Word into the fact that God is alive today. He still has His ladies at the well, His Esthers, His Moses, His Jeremiahs, and Pauls. The Book hasn't been rewritten. It is already written and is being lived out everyday as we go about our everyday business. God wants to use each and everyone of us, if we are willing to allow Him to have dominion in and over our lives. He took the prophets of the Bible times through some unbelievable things. He continues to take us through things only a child of His could or would go through. I say thank you Lord, let your will be done.

I look at all we go through, and I realize it is the Book. The Book, He said was written from the beginning, and only He can read it. He watches as we encounter all the things He already knows is going to happen. He gives us the will and the opportunity to make our own decisions, but ultimately He already knows what we're going to do. He knows who is His, and who will dedicate their whole life and heart to Him. He knows His children, as well as, when we fully accept the truth, we also know our Father, God, the Lord Almighty, the Great I Am, Jehovah. I love Him, and He alone is worthy of my love, despite any curse. I will follow Him because I know through it all He will lead and guide me to all truths. God is love. He loves me despite what or who has something negative to say about me. He is my Father, and I will follow Him until I die.

God said, we overcame them by the blood of the Lamb, and the Word of our testimony. As I look at my life, I see testimonies are my everyday walk with Him. My soul cries out "Hallelujah" because God has been so good to me. Even in the bad times, He has been the wall I lean on, and it has never fallen. He is my strength. He has never let me down. "God, you are so good."

I look at the world and all the turmoil, and I realize so many people are lost. It breaks my heart because they don't know my Father, even though, He gave His son's life to save me, you and everyone from eternal damnation. So many ignore His grace and mercy, He continues to allow to follow us every day of our lives. Tender mercies that are brand new every day.

I often get condemned for speaking about my Lord and Savior. I get called everything, but a child of God. Even that allows me to know I am His. He is my Father. Only my Father could love a child like me, I challenge Him so. I'm not perfect. He knew none of us would be, but I'm still loved by Him. He keeps His loving arms around me. I cry as I call out to Him, and He hears my cry. His Word says He will. He is God, and He cannot lie.

Let me tell you about some of the testimonies, unbelievable but real. Sometimes, I wonder if they should write appendices to the Bible. God's people need to know what the Hebrew boys encountered with their faith, we too today, can sustain the same things. I have been there. God gave me a word about the witchcraft that was against my dad, and the witches who did the awful deed. I didn't want to speak. I'm definitely not the one to confront anything. I hate to confront anyone, but the Holy Spirit that lives in me came forth and spoke out. I was physically attacked by a person who would have killed me, but the Holy Spirit came over me and as that person beat my body they did no damage, no blood, no bruises, no broken bones, nothing as I continued to praise the Lord. As the scripture states, God has given those with His spirit power to cast out demons, power to tread on serpents, and to touch deadly things and not die. He said, resist the devil, and he will flee. When I came out of the Spirit, the devil and all his demons were gone. So when you're right with Christ, He will protect you from everything, if it's in His will. It's not just a fairy tale, the Hebrew boys really did get put in the fire, and didn't get burned. Read on.

CHAPTER TWO

THE CURSE

For I, the Lord your God, am a jealous God, visiting the iniquity of the fathers upon the children to the third and fourth generations of those who hate me.
Exodus 20:5 (KJV)

I call heaven and earth as witnesses today against you, that I have set before you life and death, blessing and cursing; therefore choose life, that you and your descendants may live.
Deuteronomy 30:19 (KJV)

So many people really don't believe curses exist. Boy, how wrong they are. The Word of God tells us, the sins of our forefathers will pass through the generations. Some how in all the chaos of this world, created by the master magician himself, the devil, people weren't and still aren't paying attention. The devil appears to be winning, but it's just an illusion. It's not real because the battle is already won, and those in Christ are on the winning side. We don't have to continue to live such destructive lives.

God, the Father, His Son and His Spirit is the only answer. Only God can break a curse, however, He has placed in us His power, through the Holy Spirit, when we fully turn our life over to Him. That's all God really wants anyway. He wants us to be who He created us to be. Real. Loving. Forgiving. Authentic. His image without all the baggage handed to us by the devil, when we make what seems to be defective choices. Choices that don't seem to be in line with God's will for us.

He wants us to trust Him like Mary trusted Jesus, and He loved her. She knew when she had Him in her life, she didn't need anything else. I hate to say it, but sometimes you have to go through some things before you learn to trust God like Mary. You have to be willing to surrender all. Sometimes things get so bad, Christ is the only one you can turn to, and know He can and will deliver you from the hands of the devil. He delivered me, FINALLY. It was a curse. This curse even had a name. Rabbit, a man way ahead of his time, gave it a name. He analyzed the situations that continuously happened to people who came in contact with my sisters and I, and thereby called it the "Miller Effect."

The "Miller Effect" came from my daddy and maybe from his, or maybe it just started with him. I don't know, but it definitely started. It's a curse of promiscuity and lust. It effects the males and the females. It's a crazy sex drive. Only those that partake of the nectar, will never forget it and be permanently hooked. It's bad, and for some it's worse. The curse attracts persons who need to feed any deficiency they might have as a result of growing up in an unstable, or what the world today calls a dysfunctional family. My Spirit tells me the term dysfunctional is a lie, they're cursed and that's the truth. Wouldn't you know, my major deficiency erupted from trying to love a man who didn't love me. Lord have mercy, and He did. Thank you, Lord.

I have spent my whole life trying to love a man who wouldn't love me. I put my trust in a man. That's just it, I put my trust in. If you can't trust the people you call your parents, who can you trust? A parent's ministry is suppose to be the one that teaches you how to trust God, the Creator. So many parents have and are failing their children. So many parents don't know the truth, and the world is suffering. The devil is busy. He is constantly on his job, He'll do whatever he can to keep people from fulfilling God's purpose. When my father rejected me, I did everything I could to please him, to get his approval, to make him love me. Ultimately, he made me feel as if I wasn't good enough to be loved by him. In turn, I believed I wasn't good enough to be loved by any man. Sounds like a very low and beaten self-esteem.

That's how I became "One of Those Women". One of those women Bishop T.D. Jakes talks about in his book, and the Bible talks about in John and Joshua and many of the other books. The lady at the well, who was thirsting for something no man could ever give her. Rahab, the prostitute, who put her total confidence in a God she didn't even know. But until I knew Jesus, I mean really know Him, I kept attempting to fill that empty void with men. My substitute was men, but there are so many other counterfeits like alcohol, drugs, work, whatever the curses crave. If we can only be real, authentic, and recognize the tricks of the devil, the generational curses, the familiar spirits that follow us until the curses are broken off of us and our family's. Now, think of thirsting for something no man could ever give you, and having the generational curse of promiscuity with "fatal attraction" nectar. Lord have mercy!

The whole thing is almost unimaginable. The only thing my father seemed to love was sex, and that's all I learned might satisfy that emptiness I had inside from not being loved by that man, my earthly father. I never even had a chance. The curse killed him, so I guess, I was doomed from the beginning to be "One of Those Women." You know it only takes the truth to open your eyes to see that God is God. He is real and expects us to be real. He expects us to know that life, as we know it, is a process. He has given us the tools we need to overcome the ruler of this world, and all his devices, but there's a catch. We have to be real because the Lord is real. He can only use us when He knows we have reached a point of authenticity. The point when we have decided to LIVE in this life and enjoy the abundant life He has promised us.

The devil is a liar. My real Father said, if I trusted and believed in Him, He would deliver me from the bondage of the devil, through the curse. He allowed me to see, He could fill that void and be all I could possibly ever want or need. He allowed me to see, He could and would supply all my needs, and give me whatever I want, as long as I give Him the glory for giving it to me. He showed me that my life was not my own. He showed me, if I truly want to live this life in peace and harmony, the life He desires for me, I will have to put my total trust in Him. He told me, if I listen and follow Him, He would lead and guide me to all Truth. He told me to go forth and do His will, fulfill the purpose He sent me here for, which is to draw people to Christ. He has shown me that He has given everyone their specific means to accomplish His mission, His will, but He must be the fuel for the mission. You can't start your trip without Him. If you do dare try to get started without Him, you won't go far, and it's guaranteed to be a bumpy road, even though, we all are just roads under construction. This is my story. My toils. The curse at it's best, and my deliverance.

CHAPTER THREE

CHOSEN

For I know the thoughts that I think toward you, saith the Lord, thoughts of peace, and not of evil, to give you an expected end. Then shall you seek me and find me, when you shall search for me with all your heart. And I will be found of you, saith the Lord: I will turn away your captivity, and I will gather you from all the nations, and from all places whether I have driven you, saith the Lord; to be carried away captive.
Jeremiah 29: 11-14 (KJV)

This chapter is about Johnny, my first, and should I say, my only fiancée. I was never officially or unofficially engaged to any of the other men I encountered, even though I said, "I do" to three of them.

God told me beforehand who this book would be written about, but I seriously had to ask God what role did my relationship with Johnny play in this ministry. The curse was obvious. In fact, it was probably, the major portion of our relationship.

We both enjoyed being free. We respected each other's space

and privacy. During this time, I required a lot of space. I had a business to run and children to care for. We weren't pressed. We just enjoyed being together, in and out of bed, but mostly in bed.

He didn't even fit the profile of the man I dreamed would be in my life, but he was still all that. He looked just like Tony Dorsett, the former Dallas Cowboy, and he too was a star football player. Needless to say, he was a hulk.

This time in my life, I was really struggling with the death of my mother, and Johnny filled that void. That's only when I wasn't too busy to need him. Remember this, it has been said "busy" stands for being under satan's yoke. I was busy taking care of myself, and those left in my care. I no longer had a mother to watch over me or take care of me. That man, I tried so hard to get to love me, totally mentally abandoned us, the children, his children, left at home, leaving us motherless and you might say fatherless too.

I had a trained survival instinct, and I was surviving, very well, if I say so myself. I lived a very sinful life, lying, stealing, whoring, drugs, and crime. I had my own staff, clients, and investors too. You might have called me a little gangster child. You would never thought it, but it was real. I was living the life, money, good school grades, sports, clothes, transportation, and a man. Everything anyone would want, but wouldn't you know, God had other plans for me.

It makes me realize now that God's way shall prevail. I was Chosen. He allowed me to remember, He told me what I would be at age 9, without telling me the full story. God has been there with me and for me every step of the way.

God knew my plans were to marry Johnny, when I turned eighteen, even if I had to postpone my educational goals. I loved him, or I thought I did. I loved our relationship. He made me laugh and feel at ease with myself, but marrying him would have changed the plans God had for me, my destiny.

Johnny was killed in a car accident before my eighteenth birthday, one weekend when I was supposed to go meet his family for the first time. I don't even remember exactly when it was, even though, it was a monumental point in my life. I really did a good job of blocking the memory and the pain of my loss, the mind truly is an awesome instrument. Tears roll down my cheeks right now because I loved him and our relationship had just become committed. I feel the pain as if it happened yesterday. God it hurts.

I guess he would have been my Delilah, instead God made him my Hagar. He had to go. God wasn't honoring the illegitimate relationship. I was Chosen, and the seed God planted in me had to grow and come to fruition. God knew there was hurting people who would need to hear the truth, no matter how nasty and dirty it may be, the truth – the whole truth and nothing but the truth. The Word says, the Truth will set you free, and the truths in this book are many people's hidden secrets. But I'm here to tell you, God loves you so much. He stripped me naked for the whole world to see, despite your curse, your shortcoming. He loves you.

Now I see the picture, I know God is in control, and He will remove whatever, whomever, He has to, to accomplish His will. I say, Johnny, forgive me for being chosen and not knowing it. Even though, I don't know if I could have left him alone, even if I knew. God intended to use this story as a ministry.

God is calling His Chosen people to come forth. Like Lazarus – wake up, shake off the grave clothes, those things that hinder your way to Christ, and also those things that hinder your walk with Christ, for those who already believe. Believers, God wants to see His children evolve and come into the full knowledge of Him. He wants us to come alive, to live. He wants us to live this life to it's fullest.

I'm glad God allowed Johnny to come back to see me. He came with my mother to tell me, they were okay, and everything would be all right. God did say, weeping would only endure for a night and joy would come in the morning light. Thank you, Lord for the morning. Thank you Lord for your Light. Thank you Lord for choosing me.

Johnny, I love you, and I'll be seeing you.

CHAPTER FOUR

MARRIAGE OF CONVENIENCE

Wait on the Lord: Be of good courage, and He will strengthen thine heart: wait, I say, on the Lord.
Psalms 27: 14 (KJV)

And my God shall liberally supply (fill to the full) your every need according to His riches in glory in Christ Jesus.
Philippians 4:19 (AMP)

Even though, the theme of this book focuses on one particular curse, the curse I practiced so gracefully for many years, and the curse satan used to try to destroy my life. It was the curse that fed my insatiable lust, my bottomless pit, my void. There was other curses that also plagued my life, but I thank God, He had mercy on me, and intervened quickly with those curses.

There is a curse that has reigned in my mother's family for generations. This curse stole lives. It cut them down in their prime, and produced many motherless and fatherless children. This curse was cancer. No specific type, just cancer, all types. It was no specifically named cancer that stole my grandmother's life when my mother was 11 years old with a younger sister and three brothers to raise, and it was lung cancer that stole my mother's life, when I was 15 years old with two younger sisters and a niece to raise. The same lung cancer that has recently been attributed to breast cancer undetected since breast cancer has struck my youngest and my oldest sisters. In reality they are just curses traveling through the bloodlines, through the generations.

Yet, unlike my sisters, at 17 years of age, I was diagnosed with uterine cancer. The cancer that would render me barren. The cancer that would take away one of my life's dreams, which was to have a child of my own, to love that child and have that child love me, ultimately trying to fill my void. The cancer that would take away one of the purposes God put me here for. The cancer that would take away a woman's special treasure. I always knew I was born to have children, and raise them in the knowledge and glory of the Lord, and the curse of cancer was trying to defeat my purpose.

Seventeen years old, motherless and you might as well say fatherless, too. I was cancer stricken, and I had to make a decision. What a decision for a 17 year old to have to make alone. I knew what I wanted out of life, and I knew what my ultimate goal was, but I had to make a decision that would change my whole life. I had to decide whether I would do as the doctors planned, which was to have a hysterectomy, or what I knew I could do while I had the chance, which was to get pregnant and have a child. My gift to this world, and my gift to God. Recreate the love that can only be known and shown by a mother.

The decision wasn't particularly hard. It wasn't like I had to break my virginity or anything. Remember, I was cursed with promiscuity, and my virginity was long gone. I chose to have a child, to ride out the cancer, and pray my child wouldn't be affected. I really didn't think much about my health because the curse only affected me during my monthly flow, the scriptural curse.

I did think about my future. I had two boxes of college offers, colleges and universities all around the world, overseas and from every branch of the military. Despite my attendance record in school, I always managed to maintain my grades. I know now, that it was only God because I know all knowledge comes from Him. He always intended for me to succeed. After all, He had planted the seed of intelligence in me. No devil can take that away what God has planted in you, he can only hinder that seed from growing and coming to maturity.

I had plans to become a doctor, OB/GYN. I really didn't want anything to do with the gynecology part but at that time they had outlawed midwifery which is what God planted in my spirit. I recognized my calling and chose to be a midwife at the age of 9. Now, what 9 year old knows anything about midwifery especially in an outlawed state.

Don't you know, God had already programmed me for one of my ministries. The ministry of the unborn, ministering to mothers, and fathers too, if they are present. Ministering for nine months, teaching them about our Father. Teaching them how to enjoy the miracle God was performing in their body and how to enjoy the birthing process. Then, teaching them an art, the ministry of a mother or parent. You know, nine months is a long time to know someone as intimately as you should know the person that cares for you during the development of a life, a miracle, inside your body. Our Father has allowed me to know that this calling as a midwife is not only physical, but also spiritual. Many are becoming pregnant with fruit for the kingdom and God has sent me to help deliver these spiritual babies, ministries, callings, and gifts.

Even now, God is showing me that He has been preparing me for this ministry, so the delay was in His will because I will perform that ministry. The vision is already set. God has given me the gift of laying on hands. I've been called to bless the unborn. Even now, I see the affect of the children that are blessed in the womb, even to those parents that aren't presently in the faith. It will be their children to bring them to the fullness of the truth. After all, John did get filled in the womb and started his ministry from young. God has sent me to minister to the unborn, still protected in the womb. Their spirits will be fed and grow as their body grows, so they will remember and know God before entering this world, a world where deception began at the very beginning. God will protect them. They are His Chosen people. There's a new generation, the " Resurrection Generation," coming on board. But, they still require the prophets and the disciples of the Old Testament. That is the era we're living in now. Yes, we will be like the Old Testament to the Resurrection Generation.

That was just my Lord revealing a mystery to me, as He does often, now that I am in His will. You see, God has had this thing we call life mapped out from the beginning. If we come to the point where He can share it with us, and we are willing to submit to His gracious will, He will. He is truly a Father that will take care of you and give you what you need when He feels the time is right and He knows you are able to bear it.

Anyway, at 17, I sought out to have a child. I had a plan. I really didn't want a man, not one to keep. I still somehow intended to have the life I had envisioned for myself, but I wanted a child. So the plan was to find a married man and have his child. I wasn't going to do it under the false pretense that I wanted him, only the child. It was never my goal to break up a marriage or to be married, but God had a plan. He was preparing this ministry. The thought that all this was sinful, or adulterous, never even entered my mind. Remember, I was living a few curses, and hadn't met Christ.

I met Harold in a club one night, when my cousins convinced me to go out. I had been sitting home mourning the loss of my fiancée, Johnny, who had recently been killed in a car accident. I finally gave in and went out. Harold was a nice guy, but definitely not the one I envisioned would be the man in my life. The man in my life was to be tall, dark, slim, and an island child. I have this thing about dark men since my father, the only man I loved, was light skinned, and thought he was God's gift to the world. He made me hate the thought of light skinned men. So, as you've probably guessed, Harold was light skinned, and had a beard to go with it, definitely not me, but that was what I wanted, a man I could make a child with and not keep, not even want.

I told Harold my dilemma. He agreed to father my child, so we sought out to make a baby. Little did I know, the only child, a son, Harold called his wasn't his. It was his wife's son. He was only supporting him, even though, he really loved that little boy. If that's not bad enough, his wife was unfaithful and cheating on him, too.

I discussed the whole situation with Harold, and he agreed to everything. However, all that was going on in his life weakened him, along with the curse I possessed, and he was hooked. That sweet nectar captivated him. He decided to leave his wife, divorce her and be with me. I really didn't want that, but with all the things that transpired with me, I ended up thinking I didn't have any other choice. God, if I only knew You like I know You now. So many people would have been spared the effects of the curse. Then again, I wouldn't have this ministry to share, so others like me can see that God is the only key to unlock the door to freedom.

— *One of Those Women* —

After six months, I finally got pregnant. When I told my daddy, he wasn't particularly surprised. After all, he thought and confessed all his daughters were whores, sluts and any other not so nice words you can think of for a female. Prime example of speaking something into a life. You have to be cursed to be one of those women. The climax came when I told my daddy my pregnancy wasn't a mistake. I planned it. I made a decision. I had cancer, but cancer or no cancer, my pregnancy wasn't a mistake. Therefore, he said, he wouldn't help me. I have never regretted making that decision. My children are gifts from God, so that really didn't matter. I told him all I wanted him to do was give me my portion of my mother's social security money. That was the least he could do since he'd been using it to pay my current stepmother's rent. He said no, no without hesitation.

I was left without support for my child. I had already made an agreement with Harold. He didn't have to help me because this was my child, my choice. I released him from all obligations. Consequently, I ended up on the welfare rolls, something I thought would never happen to me. Not that I'm too proud to accept welfare, but all the means were there, so I felt I shouldn't have to go that route, and accept what I always thought of as charity. I have always worked, so I wouldn't have to take advantage of another's sweat and hard work. Since I was nine years old, I worked for my daddy in his lawn business. I always had a part time job, even if it was cleaning someone's house. I can say my dad definitely instilled a serious work ethic in all of us, and a hustling one too. So, for the first time in my life, I had to depend on something or someone other than myself or my mother to support me, because she was no longer there.

I had my child on April Fool's day. My daddy had a picnic with that. He even thought I was April fooling him. His first thought came when I told him I was in labor, and second when I told him I had a boy. He was never able to have one. I've heard it said, God gives you what you need. Lord knew he didn't need any sons to make like him, to make more women like us, his daughters. However, He gave me a son because He knew what the future would hold. I couldn't believe it when Harold questioned the paternity of his son because he looked like an Indian baby. His complexion was brown with cherry red tones, and he had a head full of long silky black hair. That particular description could fit the child of one of my ex-boyfriends. My child had a regular black Indian glow like Michael, my ex, but he wasn't Michael's baby. It didn't matter. He was my baby, my child, my gift to God and God's gift to me.

After the baby was born, the effect of the curse, the cancer, reappeared and the surgery was back on. Now, I had to live with the cancer, a father that wouldn't help me, a man who finally had a son of his own, but seriously questioned his paternity, his wife who was an adulterer, and a wicked stepmother. Could things get any worse? My dreams were shattered, and I really didn't know what to do. Even with my gift, my child, I felt so very alone, and I didn't know why.

One day, for no reason at all, I ended up in Norfolk on Church Street, which wasn't a good part of town. I ended up at a Mission there, located in one of the condemned storefront buildings. It was there, that night, that I was introduced to and Christ took my life. He saved me and through the gift of healing through the laying on of hands by Elder Luther, my body was healed of cancer. That same night, healed, filled, and baptized with His Holy Ghost.

That night when I left the mission, I lost my taste and desire for cigarettes. My thirst for the Word, for Jesus was insatiable. I went home, and I prayed that night. I really prayed. I had a peace I didn't understand, and a fear I couldn't pin down. It was in the middle of that night, my deceased mother and fiancée came to me. They came back in what appeared to be immortal flesh. They told me not to worry, everything was going to be okay, and they assured me they were okay. I loved seeing my mother again. It made me very happy, knowing my fiancée was there with her, and they were watching over me.

Then, as I lay there thinking on the Lord and all that had happened, I felt a queasing in my stomach. My belly button opened up and a white creamy liquid oozed from my body. It stank, as I got one of the baby cloths to clean it up. I had no idea what it was at the time, but I trusted that whatever it was, like my mother said, it would be all right. I experienced an unforgettable sleep, such peace is unimaginable.

I continued with the doctor's plans to have the surgery. I had all the tests repeated prior to the scheduled surgery date. Low and behold, all the tests came back negative. The doctor's just knew that couldn't be right. So, they requested all the tests again, to include the biopsies. I told them they could do all the tests, except the biopsies because they really hurt. The second set was negative too. The doctors were baffled. I testified, I had been seeing another doctor, one greater than them, the greatest of all, my Father, Jehovah Rophe, my Lord and Savior, Jesus Christ.

Jesus healed my body, and He was filling me up with His word. I was on a mission. I would go out witnessing, soul winning, with another single parent teen female almost every day. Out in the highways and byways, the outside shopping mall, telling people about Jesus and allowing them the chance to accept Him into their lives and really get to know His love. I fellowshipped almost every night. God was truly moving in the mission, and in me. You need know the demons knew what was going on because they know who Jesus is and who belongs to Him.

I was getting full in Christ. The more my spirit grew, the more the demons attacked. God was feeding me every day. He would tell me things, and show me things. Many things I didn't understand and sometimes when I went to Elder Luther, he didn't either. He would just say, wait on God, He'll reveal it to you in time. The things God showed and told me always came to fruition. Always.

For instance, God gave me three vividreams in a row. Those are very very vivid vision like dreams, three consecutive nights. The first was Jesus, Moses, and Elias up on the Mount. The next night, I saw Jesus carrying His cross, thorns in His head, beaten and brutalized body, sour wine mingled with gall, scrapped hands, scrapped knees, bloody and sweaty body. I saw Him carry the cross all the way up to Calvary. I saw them nail His wrists to the cross and His ankles too. I saw them lift the Cross as His body hung heavy, pulled by the gravity of His body weight. That was my God in the flesh, enduring the pain, for us, because He loves us that much. The last vividream was my infant son dying, being without breath or heartbeat, limp and purple. Then, God woke me up in the vividream, and gave me a prayer to pray. You must know, the last vividream scared me. It scared me really bad. That's when I had to speak to Elder Luther.

God revealed things to me about the devices of satan. He revealed to me that my daddy was indeed rooted, witchcraft, black magic, a spell. Whatever you choose to call it, it was evil at it's best. This evil was devised by my stepmother's aunt, who was the queen witch. My stepmother was one of her apprentices, and she had bewitched my daddy.

Then, one day God started bringing all the revelations to pass. I was walking through the house one day to go to the bathroom. The kitchen was full of my stepmother's cousins and relatives. Demons travel in packs. God made me stop in the middle of the kitchen and speak the revelation He had given me. It wasn't me because I wasn't the one to confront, I just now learned how to say what's on my mind, but it came straight out of my spirit. The demons got upset, Pam, my stepmother's teenage cousin, who was pregnant the same time I was and receiving financial help from my stepmother, jumped me. She was known for being bad, physically bad. She beat me with all her might. She intended to really hurt me, after all, I was talking about her mother. But the spirit of God came over me, and I didn't feel any thing. God had angels standing in the way, just like the angel that stood in the way of the donkey that spoke to the Prophet Baalam. I could see everything going on, but all I could do was shout and praise God in the spirit. I couldn't even lift my hands to fight. When I came down from my spiritual high, I was all alone. God said, resist the devil and he will flee from you. He also said, turn the other cheek. I guess that was a now time revelation of His power because that was a testimony comparable to the three Hebrew Boys, and it happened to me. I held my peace and the Lord fought my battle.

That episode was truly an act of God. It was witnessed by satan's demons. It wasn't long before the devil utilized the spell on my daddy to give me another testimony, a testimony of being homeless. Eighteen years old, infant child, one dress on my back, no job, no money in my pocket or the bank, no transportation and the sky and the stars were the roof over my head. The devil convinced my daddy, it was my stepmother or me. I came home one day to find all my things on the doorstep. Everything had been rummaged through by the demons, the scavengers, my stepmother's children, who had never had anything nice. Can you say homeless, lost and without?

Two sisters at the mission took me in, Rachael and Sarah. I went to live with them in Norfolk, in their two bedroom apartment. Kenny, my baby, and I slept with Sarah, and Rachael slept with her two daughters. They were true saints because they never asked me for anything. The people in the mission were all saints. They were all to willing to help. I never realized it until now, but they truly showed and displayed the love of Christ. The Word does say that we Christians will be known by the love we show one another. Maybe that's why the spirit truly moved in the Mission. I saw demons leave people. I mean actually see them leave their body and walk out the door. I've seen people fly in the spirit, and cars drive themselves while the occupants were in the spirit. God was moving and definitely in control.

One night in a fellowship at the mission, we were having prayer in preparation to leave when my spiritual demeanor totally changed. I found myself, Cynthia, tucked away, up in my brain, watching and feeling, but unable to respond. It felt like my body had been embalmed, lifeless. The saints at the mission said I turned an ashen gray, and my eyes, with the veins popping out of them, protruded out of my head. I stayed in that state, in the mission, for over an hour. Finally almost midnight, Elder Luther told them to take me home and keep him posted.

Harold escorted me out as we went to leave. It was a hot July night. As I left out the door, I began to breathe out frost, as if it were cold. It was cold. I was up on the mount with Moses and Elias. I was in Jesus' body, and we all talked. Then, they put me in the car. We went to the apartment, which was up, steep, narrow, dark stairs. They struggled to get me out the car. I fell to the ground. I almost had to crawl to the door. The weight was unbearable, and the sharp spikes in my head sent excruciating pain throughout my body. My hands hurt and my knees did too. My body was weak as blood oozed from my pores. I was Jesus carrying the Cross. No one knew what was going on but me and I couldn't say anything. I had to take the Cross up those steps, I could imagine how Jesus had to take it up the Hill Golgotha. I fell many times, in fact, Harold had to help me up, several times. He must have been my Simon. They really couldn't understand what was going on. I resisted going up those steps, but I continued to go. There was something strong inside of me that wouldn't allow me to stop. There was a burning deep inside me that made me press my way, as if there was a prize of some sort at the end of my journey. When I finally got to the top of the stairs, I felt the indescribable pain of having nails driven in my wrists and then my ankles. My body was so exhausted and numb from the shock of the pain. It really didn't matter anymore, until the gravity and weight pulled against my attached wrists and ankles, as they pulled the cross to an erect standing position. How could anyone suffer so, for people who deny Him every day and always have. My God, My God, what a love. I felt His compassion, as He forgave them and gave up the Ghost. God didn't allow me to give up the Ghost before he brought me out of the spirit, only to find my son, dead.

We had been home for over an hour. Sarah put Kenny to bed and laid with him until he was asleep. Then, she went to take a shower, which took all of 30 minutes. After the first two vividreams were fulfilled, I came out of the spirit, and found my lifeless child. He was purple, not breathing, limp, with no heartbeat. I grabbed him up in my arms, but he just hung there limp. His body was totally lifeless. I screamed as I gave him to Harold. He cried like a baby as he held his dead son's body. Everyone was just looking at Kenny in his daddy's arms. No one bothered to call 911. After about 30 more minutes, God's spirit came over me again, and I prayed the prayer He gave me in the third vividream, after I anointed everyone with oil. My son's life was restored. No brain damage, no defects, nothing. I knew at that point, he belonged to God. I was just the caretaker of his soul.

Even though God was doing all these miraculous things with and through me, you have to know, the curses that were over my life still existed. At that point, I didn't even know anything about curses, therefore, I never repented of them, and they continued to reign. Darrell was conceived because the curse was still working. That's when I did a lot of thinking about what would be best for me and my children. I accepted Harold's proposal to marry me. I knew it was only a marriage of convenience. I knew he wasn't the man the Lord had set apart for me, but I thought he would at least take care of me and his children. I knew in my heart, and I spoke it too, the marriage wouldn't last any longer than four or five years.

We said, "I do." It was nothing like I thought it would be. Harold didn't even trust me. He didn't trust me enough to provide a place for his family, a place of our own, for me and the boys to live. He was afraid history would repeat itself, coming home, and finding his first wife in bed with another man. Consequently, we, the children and I, moved seven times in two years, from one person's house to another.

The last stop before I stepped out on my own was Harold's parents house in Miami. Harold's daddy came onto me the second day I was there. I had never met this man before. He said he would take care of Harold's husbandly responsibilities since he wasn't there. I was terrified. Even though, I knew it was only a marriage of convenience, I did love Harold. He was the father of my children, and I knew him. I told Harold about his father, only after he asked. We had some kind of telepathic thing going on. He called from Cuba one night, He said something told him his dad was doing something to me. That let's you know God is always watching. I hadn't totally backslid at that point, but I was on my way. The forces of satan were at work to take me out. His dad even offered me money, $500 cash for five minutes of my time.

Harold's mom forced me to stay out of the house most of the time. She ensured I was fully clothed, no shorts in grand ole HOT Miami. I lost a lot of weight in five months and was in good shape. I worked out, closed up in the living room, every night. Little did I know, Harold's dad was outside peeping through the window, watching me while satisfying his lust.

Harold's parents used to trip me out because his dad was a deacon and his mother was a deaconess in the community church. The Long family was the pillar of society, but when it all hit the fan and all the secrets came out, it was a mess.

There was much craziness in this family. Harold's dad tried to sleep with his own daughter. Harold's mom kept trying to get at me and the girl down the street because she thought he was messing around with one of us. All the time, he was trying to keep it in the house, so no one would know the deep dark sin and perverted lust that embedded itself in his heart.

That whole episode came to a close when Harold's mom sliced my throat in an attempt to kill me. I thank God Harold's dad rescued me. He grabbed the knife from Ms. Lillie's hand before it went too deep. I didn't even try to stop her. I still don't understand that, but I made it my business to get out of there in a hurry. So, I went back home to my daddy's house. That was the first time my dad was there for me, or ever took up for me. I still can't believe the blatant hypocrisy of the Long family.

I went home and started my life all over again. God blessed me with a roof over my head, transportation and enabled me to go back to school. I was doing fine by myself. I don't know whether to blame it on my heart, always feeling sorry for people, or the curse, but I took Harold back into my life.

Things were good for a little bit. Harold still didn't trust me though, and that made life miserable. I was on a time clock for everything, even to go to the grocery store, a place that always fascinates me, and he knew it. That's when the physical abuse started. I fought Harold from the beginning, after all, I really didn't love him like that. It was just a marriage of convenience.

Then the curse kicked in, even though I had made up my mind I would learn to love Harold like that, and be a wife to him. Harold was on night shift, and I started going out. It was on. I never got caught, it just seemed to be something to do.

After a couple of months of misery, the damn broke. My Cinderella stepmother snitched, and I had the police tracking me down with a warrant for my arrest. I listened to my stepmother and was receiving benefits from the social service system, yet I was still married to and living with Harold. He was right there, and very aware of my indiscretions, enjoying the extras.

I hid from the police for months, until we, Harold and I, decided it would be best for me to join the military. We couldn't afford to repay the monetary values of the benefits received, and I didn't want to go to jail. I could and would do a lot of things, but jail wasn't one of them.

It had to be God's will because I was really overweight and had to loose thirty pounds before I could enter the military and go anywhere. Then, I could only get into the Army. I had too many dependents for any other branch. It only took me a month to get down to size, then I left.

I left my children to escape punishment. I never meant to abandon them or be alienated from them, which is what happened. Harold started to turn away from me immediately after I left. He changed his mind about our decision for me to go into the military, but I had already sworn in. It was too late. I was left alone to face this by myself.

Basic Combat Training (BCT) was a trip. Before I even got that far, I was held over. My pregnancy test was positive. I wasn't pregnant. I just had an IUD removed, and the baby I was carrying with the IUD misaborted. I had to wait until the test came back negative before I could go forward. Of course, Harold used that to say I aborted the baby because it wasn't his, not so.

At BCT, all the drill sergeants were trying to holla at me. One of the soldiers got court martialed when he over stepped his ground trying to get with me. I telephoned home often, but

Harold wouldn't allow me to talk to the boys. That really hurt me, but there was nothing I could do. I was in training, but even that didn't stop the curse. It was at large as usual. This time, it got me my rights read to me. Fraternization is what it's called in the military, and I was in the Army now. But as usual, my Lord protected me from their punishment. He had his own to come.

I didn't graduate BCT with all the other troops. I was held over again. This time to wait for the court martial to take place. I was stuck at Fort Dix, until I went to my Advanced Individual Training (AIT). AIT was a party. I was on my own for the very first time. No, that's not totally true. I was just without people around me I knew. I've always been on my own, only I always had an audience. Harold did everything to keep me away. I had to beg to come home and see my children. I just found out about two years ago, Harold had another woman, his wife now, while I was at BCT. No one is free from satan's traps.

I was drawn out. I was totally back in sin. The man I said "I do" to had someone else. I was cursed, and my family was torn apart. Can we say backslidden? I lost my focus. I was empty, and following after my own lust and desires. I was feeding my flesh. Really fleshing out.

You need to know, when you start walking after the flesh, after your own desires, things go wrong because they are wrong. God did say, there was nothing good in this flesh. Sure God will ultimately use any situation for His good, but it's not good for you. You sure won't think it is because you'll pay for your wrong doings. Yes, you'll pay for ALL your wrong doings and turning your back on Christ is definitely wrong. You'll pay, that's for certain. He says He chastises those that are His. It's just like a parent chastising their child, only all God's chastisement is well thought out, and you never know how He's coming. There's always a lesson to be learned, if you open your spirit and receive it. Then, God will try you again. There's always a test.

The test to see whether or not you actually learned your lesson. If you pass, like school, you go to the next level. There's always another level in Christ. You are always evolving, until you go to sleep or onto the ultimate level in flight, the last flight, with Him in the Rapture.

My ultimate desire was triggered by the curse, the curse of promiscuity. I paid for being ignorant of the sins of my forefathers, my ancestors. Family is important to me, and mine was destroyed. Harold played hide and seek with my sons for five years. My sons thought I was dead. Until this day, they still harbor unacknowledged resentment for me not being there with them, and my having more children. I had to have children. That's is a great portion of my ministry. My sons still question whether I abandoned them. NO, NO, NO, I didn't. I love my children. I gave up the mind portion of my true being, the intellect, the education, to fulfill a goal for my Father, to be fruitful and multiply, even with all the odds against me. Remember, I was only eighteen, and I had cancer of the uterus. I chose to have my children. They are my gifts to God, from God. I would never abandon them. It still hurts sometimes when I think about those years. My eyes tear, as they are now because no one should play games with a child's heart. As a mother, my own heart was broken. I could do nothing for my children. I had no idea where, or how they were.

Yes, Harold, may have hurt me, but more so, he hurt our sons. All this pain stemmed from a curse. Darrell, today, still harbors resentment, and is on a mission to fill his void. I just wish I could tell him to trust me while I share with him and my grandchildren, my Father's love, so their void too may be filled. The children of today deserve so much more than we've been able to give them. I was lost, but now I'm found. You better watch out satan, it's on. Like Detrick Haddon says, "satan we're gonna tear your kingdom down."

CHAPTER FIVE

MARRIED TO A BACKSLIDER

Make no friendship with an angry man; and with a furious man thou shalt not go: Lest thou learn his ways, and give a snare to thy soul.
Proverbs 22:24,25 (KJV)

I will save them from all their sinful backsliding, and I will cleanse them. They will be my people, and I will be their God.
Ezekiel 37:23 (NIV)

Turn, O backsliding children, saith the Lord; for I am married unto you: and I will take you one of a city, and two of a family, and I will bring you to Zion.
Jeremiah 3:14 (KJV)

You probably think by the title I'm talking about someone else, but when I say married to a backslider, I'm talking about me. Sometimes, no, all the time, you must be careful who you connect yourself with because it might be a child of God in a backslidden state, and you'll receive the repercussions of their state. You have to think about the people you meet. You really don't know what you might be getting yourself into. I guess that's why God created discernment.

I was a backslider. I met Christ, surrendered my life to Him, was healed of cancer, and I went back out. I knew Christ for many great testimonies, but I felt like I had been trapped all my life, so I went back out. I've never had a life when I was on my own. It always seemed like I was raising someone. Always. I've been raising people all my life, and I wanted to be free. God was at work here too because, it's all been a ministry.

I tell everyone I joined the military because it kept me from going to jail. Realistically, that is true, even though, the military didn't know it. It was as if I gave up one whole life for another. It was almost as if I had too. No forces stopped me. It just happened. I don't know, maybe it was to bloom this ministry because God knows what I've been through really hurt me. Fourteen years with a man, I said "I do" too, but I was never, legally or spiritually, married to him. A man that was utterly filled with things he needed to be delivered from, and he has been a great part of my ministry. Truth be told, that's what we're all called to do. Minister the ministry of reconciliation. After all, I am a child of God. Sometimes, I wonder if I just added to his misery, or if it was indeed a ministry. I wonder sometimes, but all in all, the Word says, what the devil meant for evil, God will make good.

I have reached a plateau, and my spirit tells me Monroe is on his way. He will see life here. It may not be a long life, but it will be here in this world. Monroe did much damage. You see, the things we do in this life to damage the body, the temple of God, which can only sustain so much, after all it's made of dirt, can have drastic results. You don't even give yourself a chance when you tear down this physical body. You may have to go to sleep. Hallelujah! Thank you Lord, that even in that state, if we have become yours, we will still be yours. We will just be put to sleep, to be cleaned up, until He comes. That's pretty good. A long night's rest because God knows surviving in this life is hard work.

I was married to a man, but I wasn't married to him, for fourteen years. I paid for my backsliding. I endured utter hell. I paid for my backsliding. God says, He chastises those that are His. It was His ministry. It was a ministry of chastisement, at least that's the way I took it. An ultimate mark of His love.

It was also a ministry to show Monroe the way to Christ because he needed to know. He really needed to know, but everyone really needs to know. So, if you accept Him into your life, that's what we're here for. God said He wished all would come unto repentance, and I believe He wants all His children to be saved, but of course, some won't be. Some will only enjoy what this life has to offer. The funny thing, which really isn't funny, is, to know God is to enjoy all this life has to offer without the struggle, or the strength, the joy, and the peace to endure the struggle. It's all His, and He said no good thing would He withhold from you. You just have to come to the point where you love Him more than you love anything or anybody in this world.

Understand me, when I say this world, I mean, that's what has to be in your mind, your body, your soul, and your spirit. This world. It's all His. If He wants you to have the whole block, it can be yours. If you can imagine that, because it's all up to you. You make the choice. If you want to live in a hut, you can live in a hut. If you want to live in a mansion, a big house, you can live there too. It's up to you. He'll give you what you can imagine, up to what you can handle because He knows what you can withstand. He said He would put no more on you than you can bear. He also said, He'd give you the desires of your heart. He puts the desire there, you realize it and that becomes your desire, your vision, your dream, your goal, His purpose for you in this life.

I keep deviating, but it's all been a ministry. Fourteen years. From day one, I should have known it wasn't right. This was a man who couldn't even say the wedding vows. The preacher had to ask him to speak up, and he was standing less than two feet from him, no less than that, maybe even a foot, after all, it was a house wedding. I couldn't even hear him, and I was standing right in front of him. My knees shook, and my hands trembled. It was such uncertainty in my spirit, it overtook my body. I really wasn't uncertain in my desire, but you have to know my desires weren't from God. I was in a backslidden state, and no one knew but me and God. Even then, God was trying to signal me that it wasn't right, but I did it anyway. They say love is blind, and you would only have to see Monroe once to agree totally with that statement.

The spirit must have seen the spirit, the truth. He didn't say the marriage vows, and then it started. Day one, he didn't come home on our wedding night. He spent our wedding night with another female, his ex-fiancée's best friend. I still don't understand their relationship. He walked her home and never came back, and I waited. All night, I waited. In the living room chair, fully dressed, no less, I waited. I couldn't go to bed because his ex-fiancée was upstairs in the bed we normally occupied. They say she was mourning the loss. She better thank God, it was her loss because I do believe only a child of God could endure the trials and tribulations Monroe had in store for whoever attached themselves to him.

Then, the journey began. Apart, we did great. We spent our first six months apart. He was in Korea, and Ebony, our daughter, and I were in Colorado. I guess, he was doing his own thing, but he would send the money. He did provide, when we were apart, but when we got together physically, he started practicing his family curse, abuse. Abuse with all the headings.

Monroe was an angry person. The anger he held within him was projected on me, physically and mentally. We're talking about injuries here. We're talking about many occasions, many, many, many occasions. Broken ribs, broken jaw, broken finger, burned arm, black eyes, and torn skin. Yes, we're talking about being kicked, punched, held hostage with a knife at your throat, slapped and even beaten while I was pregnant. We're talking pain here. Out right, physical abuse.

For a long time, I took it because I was afraid to fight back. Then God allowed me to see He wasn't going to let him kill me, so I might as well fight back, and that's exactly what I did. With all due respect, our last fight, I beat his tail. He'll claim, he wasn't really fighting, but there's no such thing as an abuser who's not really fighting. They either are or they aren't, and I beat his tail. God has put a lot in me, and like David, with Goliath, He was my deliverer. It truly was physical abuse.

Now, let's look at the neglect. I wonder, do I tie the neglect in with the mental abuse? No, we'll just go plain neglect. It was neglect for me because when you call yourself married and you decide to be else where, doing other things, with someone else, that you should be doing with your wife, you're neglecting her. You're neglecting your children for the same reason. If you're not there for your wife, you can't be there for the children, and someone has to be there for the children. It sure wasn't him, so it had to be me. Neglect for his responsibilities, when he started running around. Everything was getting messed up because he was all tied up in things, drugs, alcohol, other women, partying, and just hanging out. He was neglecting his responsibilities. He neglected supporting and providing for his family because he was too busy doing whatever he was doing. God would call him an infidel. Plain and simple, he just neglected me and the children, his family. He also neglected himself by doing the things he was doing. It was neglect, just plain ole neglect.

Then, there was mental abuse, being called everything, and being accused of everything. The only thing about this is, he never accused me of running around, but low and behold, I was cursed. If you want to say, he who is without sin, cast the first stone. I can't cast any stones. I was cursed, that dreaded curse of promiscuity. So what does that tell you?

It's the mental abuse that almost wore me down, even though, there really wasn't much mental abuse. The only mental abuse presented itself by him using the things he knew really meant something to me. After all, I was raised in a stoic household, so feelings weren't something I really knew anything about, until he kidnapped our children and held them for ransom while he spent the time and the money, hundreds of miles away, with his ex-fiancée. He knew my children meant the world to me. Then he would talk about my God. We went through some things, we should not have survived. Every time, out of no where, something always came through. No, it wasn't out of no where, it was my Father, my God, Jesus. They say, He's married to a backslider. He really is because He took care of me and my children. You can believe it. Even so, Monroe didn't know he was married to a backslider. So, he didn't know where all the goodies were coming from. I guess he thought I had it like that. I did work really hard, but I didn't have it like that. My Father took care of me. He made sure we had everything we needed when we needed it, and He still does.

I've been through some things. I really have. Fourteen years with Monroe who is a substance abuser. He even taught me how to abuse substances I didn't already abuse. He used his substance abuse to fill the void in his life, which was not being loved. That's basically a void we all have, not being loved, because you don't really know how to love or receive love until you establish a relationship with our Father, and know His love. Once you are loved by Him, oh God, there is no love like it. The Word says, husbands love your wives as Christ loves the church, but how can they, if they don't know the Father. It takes two, Christ and the church. So, you really have to know what love is to be able to give it or receive it. It's like saying, you can swim, but you've never been in water. I don't think so. So, with a husband and a wife, until you have Christ in your life, you can't know that kind of love. That kind of love is deep. Real deep. There is no love like it. There's nothing to compare it with, but it's the greatest because that love allowed God, the Father, to give His only son to be crucified for us. I sit here, and recount the pain of the abuse I suffered, I'm sure it can't touch the pain the Lord must have felt going to the cross and being crucified for people He knew was unworthy, but loved still the same by our Father, God.

 I endured because I believed God's word. I believed all those scriptures in Ephesians and Corinthians, and all the other marriage scriptures in the Bible. I believed them for what they literally were. I truly believed them, so I wouldn't give up. But without God revealing it to you, you would believe them too. I still believe them, I'm not saying I don't believe God's word, I'm just saying they have to be taken in the right context. If you don't put them in the right context, you're not believing the correct thing. God must reveal His Word to you, reveal Himself to you, and He will when you receive His spirit and decide to trust Him and walk in His way living in His will.

 I went through those wedding vows, and I stuck it out because of them. But God, finally told me, "That's not your husband." We would always end up apart then back together, apart and back together, apart and back together. It was never right. Then one day, God just said, "That's not your husband."

— One of Those Women —

I was in the midst of a sanctuary. The speaker, an anointed elder, had everyone coming up to the altar to lay hands on them. I don't even think the sermon had been preached yet, but everyone was coming. The spirit was really moving. I went up there to the altar. The spirit really moved in me, and I was truly blessed. There's nothing like a good shout. Then, I sat down, and watched the glory of the Lord. I saw the spirit move people I had never seen it move before. People who didn't believe the spirit can move you the way it moves me, all over the place, but they were moving that night.

I was just sitting there in the pew, and out of no where, I heard a voice. It was perfectly audible to me. I looked up to see where the voice came from. It was straight to the point. It said, "That's not your husband." I looked around, but I really didn't pay much attention to the voice, at first. I continued to try to get into the praise, but I couldn't. After about ten minutes, I heard it again. He said, "That's right, Monroe is not your husband." I said, "Okay Lord, so what do you want me to do?" He said, "Put him out your bed." I said, "Okay." But after a second thought, I said, "I can't do that, I don't have the heart to do that. I'll get out the bed." He didn't say anything else.

I went home. It was about 1:30 in the morning. It was late, and he was already in bed. He didn't go to church with me, although he was professing Christ. I came in the room, went down on my knees and prayed. Then I said, "Monroe, wouldn't you like to know what God told me?" He really wasn't interested. I said, "I think you'd like to know." I said, "God told me, you're not my husband, and to put you out of my bed, but I can't do that, so you can stay in the bed, and I'll sleep some place else. " Then I changed my clothes and left the room.

I went in the bathroom, and cried out to God. The bathroom was my secret closet, where I had been meeting my Father since Monroe managed to move back into my life. When I left the room, Monroe got up in a fury and started going off. You have to know, the devil was mad. God had unveiled his plot. I continued to cry out to God. Then God said, "I told you to put him out your bed, you need to be obedient." After having God chastise me, I came out the bathroom. Monroe was up. So I said, "Since you're already up, God told me to be obedient and put you out my bed, so you need to go sleep in the den." He was really torn up then. satan was mad.

Eventually other things evolved. He was still in the house, but I no longer saw him as my husband, and I treated him that way. I remember, he asked me to buy someone on his job a Christmas gift, and I didn't. So, he cut up my wardrobe. To tell you the truth, that was the first sermon I ever preached. I had a solo audience. I preached to my daughter.

God fed me that whole night. I couldn't sleep. He told me some thing's. He was really revealing some thing's to me. Then, I woke up about 4:00 o'clock that morning . I was having devotions, so I just decided to get up. I felt really good in my spirit. I didn't understand it, but I just felt really good. Then, God told me, "Put him out, put him out today." I said, "Okay Lord. I want to be obedient, this time, the first time." So, I called Deacon Patrick, Monroe's spiritual counselor, and I told him, "God told me to put Monroe out. He told me to put him out today, and I want you to come over before church and be here, if you don't mind." He said, "Fine, I'll come over." In the midst of all this, I continued in my praise, and continued with my sermon.

I went to get dressed. My hand reached for a dress, not the dress I was going to wear, however, the dress I pulled out was cut up. So, I pulled out another, and it was cut up too. I just continued to praise God. My daughter asked me to pull out another outfit, her favorite. It too was cut up, then she was upset.

At that point, I hadn't even told Monroe I was going to put

him out. I just started laying the clothes out on the living room chair, all of them. Deacon Patrick came up in the midst of me moving clothes and my sermon. I was still preaching, still praising God. I guess I was loud because Deacon Patrick said I could be heard outside. Then, Monroe walked into the living room just as Deacon Patrick came in the house. Speaking to Monroe, I said, "You have to go. You have to go today. You can't stay here any longer." I really was nice, which is unusual because we always fought, especially verbally, and this was something to fight about, unless you know who your Provider is. He wasn't willing to go. He said, he couldn't get his stuff packed and moved that quickly, but I knew better than that. I used to pack his stuff all the time, when he was caught in his many indiscretions. It never took me more than a few hours, and I would have it packed, neatly packed.

I said to everyone, "No, that's not true. He's just trying to stay, but God said, he has to leave, he has to leave today, and I have to be obedient." So, we made an agreement. I was going to church. He had to leave the house, hopefully to go to church also. Then, we would meet back at the house with Deacon Patrick. Deacon Patrick said he'd bring a vehicle to get him moved, and he would be out that day. He didn't come to church, but he didn't come back to the house either.

I wasn't going to wait around for him. My waiting days were over. The girls and I wanted to do something that day, and waiting for him wasn't in the plan. It was Sunday afternoon, and God wants us to enjoy the day we're suppose to use to rest. Rest doesn't necessarily mean laying in your bed. It may be just convening with nature, relaxing your body, relaxing your mind, just enjoying our Father and all He has made for us to enjoy.

So, we packed his stuff, the girls and I. We boxed it, labeled it, and stacked it neatly outside in the corridor. We took pictures of the stacked boxes, so he couldn't say he didn't get his stuff, just in case something should disappear. If so, I could file a claim on it. I'm always thinking. I told you, my daddy taught me well.

He had to go, but you should know, he wasn't going without trying to make me look bad. He called Chaplain Samson, my Pastor. He told him what I said. You must know, Chaplain Samson is all about saving marriages. I guess this was a revelation to him too. Maybe he believed those marriage scriptures just the way they are written. Now that I look at it, if you can believe them the way they are written, why would you need God, or the Holy Ghost, to give you understanding? All you'd have to do is read the Bible. Many people, saved and unsaved, read the Bible. They read it every day.

Those scriptures are really deeper than that. God presented this scriptural dilemma to my Pastor. He asked me about it, and I told him. I told him, "God told me, Monroe wasn't my husband." He replied, "God told you that?" I said, "Yes." He said, "I think you ought to pray to the Alpha and the Omega God, and ask Him if He truly told you that." I said, "I can do that."

Wouldn't you know, the timing was perfect. God had set me up. You see, I was scheduled to make a trip to my home town, and most of my revelations come when I'm on a journey, just driving somewhere. Maybe, I need to take more drives. I don't know.

So, I went on my journey. At this point, my Pastor is questioning me, and I'm questioning God. I asked God if what I heard was for real. I began my journey speaking to the Lord and listening to some taped gospel messages. I said, "Lord, you know I need to hear a word from you. You know I do."

It was December, when I made this trip home. It was around the time of my birthday, and my son, Kenny, had a gift for me. The Word I received from God while I was driving was "Oh ye of little faith," because I was doubting my Shepherd's voice. My son came over to where I was staying with my birthday gift in his hands. It wasn't wrapped. He said, "I'm sorry Mom, I didn't have time to wrap it, but I want to give you your birthday gift." It was a black Last Supper, a 16x20 picture. I have many pictures of the Last Supper in my house. Then, he said, "Mom, do you know what Jesus said to this one?" as he pointed to one of the disciples. Then, he said, "Jesus said, Oh ye of little faith." All I could do was praise God, praise Him with a Hallelujah, thank you Jesus! That was confirmation. "Oh ye of little faith." I said, "You know that was confirmation. Thank you Lord for speaking to me. Thank you."

So, I decided to fast and pray, still waiting on an answer from God because that let me know what I heard was from God. I told God, I want the rest of it. I need an explanation because I'm going to have to go there.

God gave me John 4:15. It's about the Samaritan woman at the well. Jesus told her to go get her husband. She told him, Lord I have no husband. He said to her, you have answered correctly because you had five husbands, and the one you're with now is not your husband. Then, He went on to say to me, "Yes, I am the Alpha and the Omega. I am God. I lie not. I am the Beginning. I am the End. I am that which was, that which is, and that which shall be. I said it then, and I'm saying it now, Monroe is NOT your husband."

All I could do was praise Him. Then, I said, "Lord, I don't want to seem disobedient. You know, if I have to choose between man and God, I have to choose you, God. So, Lord, please tell one of your two men of God who is familiar with my situation, Reverend Paul, or Chaplain Samson." I left it at that and continued to praise Him.

I continued in the flow of the Lord, as I went back home. I arrived home late Saturday night, but I went to church Sunday. That day, Chaplain Samson had the congregation buddy praying. He had us holding each other's hands, just two people. The person I was praying with got slain in the spirit, and God made me stumble out into the aisle. I was in a drunken stupor, a state I have never been in before in the spirit, that is, as I stumbled up to the altar. God had me fall at Chaplain Samson's feet, where he laid hands on me. Mind you, I've never known Chaplain Samson to lay hands on anyone unless he was led by God to do so. As he laid hands on me, he prayed a prayer of confirmation. I heard it in my spirit, but I didn't get a chance to talk to him about it that day.

That next Tuesday, I went to the Chaplain's office. I had to ask him what he meant by that prayer of confirmation, even though, I already knew. He said, "You know I'm against breaking up marriages, but I have to go with what God tells me. He didn't tell me like He told you, but He said, your marriage is over, and you need to get out of it quickly."

All I could say was thank you Lord. Thank you, and I commenced to doing just that. Don't you know, when God reveals something to you, then comes the test, which is usually the enemy just trying to deter you from God's will. Monroe did everything he could to take me out. He felt I was at war with him, even though, I really wasn't. For a while, I was handling things on my own, money, lawyers, time, but that didn't go well. It was a long battle. Finally, I came in the correct light with God. I let go, and let God fight my battle, even though, Monroe was still in the midst of what he was in the midst of. He was an angry person. He was killing himself, but he had met God. I thank the Lord through me, he met Him, only he hasn't come to the fullness yet.

However, at this point in time, God is working with him, to bring him to the fullness. My prayers, that agape love inside me, go out to him, as does his children's prayers. We pray he will be able to live in this life, and smell the roses. You see, even when I didn't know I was ministering, and it didn't seem like I was in

God's will, I realize now God was there using me. I guess that was like Jeremiah when he was in his backslidden stage. He said the anointing is, present tense, like fire shut up in his bones. When Monroe was going through one of his many rehabilitation trips, when the children were really young. I made him a collage. On that collage, I was ministering, seriously ministering. There was several verses on the picture that truly ministered. Verses like, "When confronted with a foe, praise him, bless him, let him go." Indeed that was a ministry because indeed, none of those things are of God, those things that ultimately tear people down. Things like anger, guilt, frustration, wanting, needing, being unloved, feeling abused, blame, all those things, and the like, are foes to us. You must know, the devil is a spirit, so he attacks the mind. He uses those foes, but God called His children to have joy and peace. Monroe was living with a lot of anger and many of the other foes I mentioned. He absorbed his infirmities in his body, and then took them out on me. The only thing about that is, God gives us this body for a short time and once you eat it up and kill it with your foes, it's gone. That's the real reason some people don't get a chance to really live in this life. They're still saved and going home to be with the Father, but they'll be put to sleep because they never gave God the chance to help them overcome. They never give Him a chance to fill the void, the emptiness, that insatiable thirst of the spirit. They never came to the full knowledge of the truth. God has the power, if you seek and find the truth, to deliver you from all that. He has the power because He made the body, and there isn't anything He can't and won't do to deliver you, if you allow Him too. I believe God because He is God, and my testimonies go to prove that fact. Ain't NOTHING He can't do.

    I said I wasn't going to go here, but my spirit tells me I should since it's early in the book. Like John the Baptist, I didn't give my life to Christ. I really knew nothing of Him. Yes, I went to church and Sunday school when I was little, but I don't ever remember being introduced to Christ. Yes, He snatched my life. He took control, but not total control. I still had a choice. I still had a will. I still had curses. Yes, He took my life. He literally healed my body of cancer. He literally took my son's life, in physical death, and gave it back to him. He let me literally be beaten and not feel a thing. He let me be literally baptized in fire, and not get burned up. He literally let me be homeless.

Now that I look at my life, and I see He has given back what the devil stole from me and more. He has given me a home where I have more rooms than I have people to put in them. I have a yard that is a lawn on one side and landscaped vegetation on the other side, manicured woodland in suburbia. I give God all the glory. He is literally spelled out in my front yard. Really spelled out, J-E-S-U-S, in His purple robe of majesty. Then, there's the Hall of Fame, Adam, Eve, Mark, Luke and more with the Great I Am at the gateway to my brick patio. Everything in the house represents Him because it's all His. The walls minister Him. He has given me top of the line vehicles. I didn't realize it, but all the gospel singers talk about riding around in their Jeep. That must be God's vehicle, a Jeep Grand Cherokee Laredo. I went and looked at the sticker price because I really didn't know what God had given me. I priced a new one, not looking to buy, but I had to take the Jeep to the shop to get rid of the last mark of the devil. $34,000. That's a whole lot, but really it isn't because God just wrote off a debt for $35,000 for me. Yes, He did. He just wrote it off. The company sent a letter saying zero balance. That's my Father, because He said, He gave me my house. No Charge. Jesus already paid the price. It all belongs to Him. Then, the personal property tax came in, $607, but I got a receipt from the city yesterday. Zero balance, and I didn't pay a nickel.

God is really good, as long as you're following Him and doing what you're suppose to do in Him. I thank God, He is allowing Monroe to see the light. I thank Him, He has allowed him to marry and start fulfilling his purpose as I am fulfilling mine. So, that's what it's like being married to a backslider. Beware, you might be saying "I Do" to an espoused child of God. If you're saying "I Do" to a child of God, and you're not of God, and it's not of God, then you're going to go through some struggles. Things are going to be revealed. God chastises those that are His. It's only because He loves you. The same way we do our children. We do it all for the good of them, so maybe they'll learn a lesson. Every day in Christ is just another day in school with God as the teacher. Out of all these things I've been through, I've learned many lessons.

I've learned there are boundaries, and no one has the right to break my boundaries, once I establish them. I've learned I have a choice. I choose whatever steps I take. However, today, I no longer have the greatest choice of all. I made that choice. It's actually the last choice I'll ever have to make on my own. The choice I made was to surrender my life, and trust God in everything I do. I will walk in Him. He will lead and guide me whichever way I go. So, I have relinquished my choice to my Lord, God, my Savior, my Father. My life belongs to Him. Thank you Lord.

CHAPTER SIX

MY SPIRITUAL WEDDING

*Whoso findeth a wife findeth a good thing,
and obtaineth favour of the Lord.*
Proverbs 18:22 (KJV)

*Enjoy life with the woman whom you love all the days
of your fleeting life which He has given to you under
the sun; for this is your reward in life, and in your toll
in which you have labored under the sun.*
Ecclesiastes 9:9 (NAS)

A double minded man is unstable in all his ways.
James 1:8 (KJV)

I was quite content, or at least I thought I was. I had everything I could ever want and dream of. God was covering me in His peace and His joy was my strength. I was blessed, and it looked like nothing could go wrong. Everything was so right.

I had just been spiritually wed to the man of my dreams, the man I wanted to spend the rest of my life with. I took it in faith that God had joined us together, and we had our own marital ceremony. Right there in my house. We exchanged rings, cheap, but it didn't matter. It was the meaning, and the motive behind the exchange. It wasn't legal, but it wasn't just a simple "I do." At that time, it couldn't be legal, or at least that's what I thought, because I had not settled my obligation to Monroe. However, it was more binding than any legal ceremony could ever be because in the depths of my soul, I was more satisfied than any person who may have had a million dollar wedding and twenty pieces of certified paper. I knew it didn't take an official for God to join two together, only to make it legal. I was convinced John was my husband. I loved him in every capacity. It was beautiful. For the first time, John dropped that male guardrail and assured me I would be his love and the lady of his life forever.

I lived in this state of bliss for some time until I felt I couldn't contain the secrecy of my happiness. The marriage was a secret because I hadn't shared this all too precious moment with my Pastor, Chaplain Samson, the one God fed for me. It seemed as if I was playing the disobedient child, trying to hide something from a parent. Yet, it was more sinister than that because God made him the caretaker of my spirit. Somehow, I knew he already knew. It was an unction from the Holy Ghost, but I knew I still had to be the one to tell him.

For the first time, I was fearful of talking to him, telling him about my marriage. Although, it was only spiritual, it really was more significant than any legal wedding without God because it was joined together and blessed by God. God made us one. I knew it was an Adam and Eve relationship, bone of his bone and flesh of his flesh.

There was a question I knew would arise, and I knew the answer I truly didn't have to give him. You're probably asking, what question? The only question my saved, sanctified, Holy Ghost filled and fire baptized Pastor would ask. Was he saved? Were we equal in yoke? Honestly, I couldn't say yes.

    I thought heavily about John's salvation. I knew he knew the Word. I knew he was raised in the church and attended a church school, and his mother is a practicing Christian. I knew he didn't want to go to church, the building. He said, when he did go, it would change his whole life forever. I knew he said he met God on the basketball court every Sunday morning, and that was his place of worship, his place of solace. I knew he lived his life as a good and righteous person and could very easily appear to be saved. I had never heard him confess salvation, although I knew he loved God, and lived by his commandments. I knew he never hindered my walk in Christ, and did all he could to promote it. I guess if I had to judge a tree by the fruit it bears, I would have to say his fruit was of God, I just never heard him confess it.

    My constant thoughts about what we had done brought about questions of my own, which planted seeds of doubt in my spirit. I was loosing faith, what might be called wavering. I questioned whether I forced John's hand to fulfill my own selfish desire and impatience to wait on God. I questioned whether the comfort and peace I felt in my spirit about being betrothed to John and being with him forever, even if it meant I had to wait seven years to physically be with him, was truly of God. Also the fact that I hadn't told my Pastor, made me doubt even more. All these factors caused confusion in my soul, knowing God is not the author of confusion, I struggled in my spirit.

    I thought heavily about how I would tell Chaplain Samson. I started by using the mechanism that seems to work best in our congregation, gossip. Even though, I don't do it, I know the ones that do. So, I presented my case to one of the ministers of the church. I presented the wedding pictures we had taken. They were beautiful, but that didn't work because that particular minister wasn't in the clique, and wasn't going to spread this gossip. They were concerned about my secrecy, and the fact that I had not consulted Chaplain Samson.

Then, I did the next best thing. I told the first lady, even though, she's definitely not one to gossip, not even to her husband. She just wanted to know how I came to the conclusion, John was my husband. She listened, but really gave no clear comment, except I must tell Chaplain Samson. I hoped I would receive some insight from her. I guess it was between me, my Pastor and God.

I still felt good in my spirit about the wedding, but I was also still uneasy about not telling Chaplain Samson. I tried to tell him New Year's night when everyone was fellowshipping, but it wasn't the right time or place. It was dinner, no breakfast, and it really wasn't the time to be counseling me. Later, there was a ministry meeting for all the leaders of the church, and I continued to be convicted in my spirit. I couldn't even look my Pastor in the eyes because I was being deceitful. Secrets are definitely a form of deception. I could tell he knew something, but he wasn't going to come to me. Then, the time came for reconciling with anyone you felt you had betrayed, and the Lord led me immediately to my Pastor. He said he already knew. No one told him. It was our Father. He said, our Father told him not to come to me, but wait for me to come. I felt so bad. All I could do was cry in his arms as he chastised me, and asked that question I feared the most. Is he saved? Like I said before, I couldn't honestly answer. Then, he said, "You know, if he's not saved, God had nothing to do with that marriage or whatever it was, and you need to come see me."

I felt bad about hearing that my spiritual marriage to the man I truly love and want to spend the rest of my life with may not be of God, but I was totally relieved and at peace about being reconciled with my Pastor. I knew God would use him to give me what I needed not to be confused.

Now, what was I going to do? The man, I called my husband in faith may not be my husband. I didn't want to force John into a spiritual corner because I knew his heart belonged to the Lord, but God had to call him to the altar on His own time. I couldn't rush him or press him into confessing salvation, especially, since we had at least three years for God to work on both of us, building and making us into who He wants us to be, single, whole, and unique individuals with a purpose. John had already allowed me to know that one trip to the right fellowship would change his whole life, which tells me God has already placed a call on his life, and was only waiting for him to answer it. I also knew that being with me, and my being "Sold Out," he would have no other choice but to give his life to Christ in the total and true sense of salvation.

You know, it really doesn't matter because John is my heart. I never knew I could love anyone the way I love him. So, what would I do? Ask my Father? That seemed to be the right thing to do. Just ask my Father to tell me who my husband is. After all, He did say cast your cares upon Him because He cares for you.

CHAPTER SEVEN

SATAN'S DEMONIC DEVICES

...and they came to the woman by night: and he said, I pray thee, divine unto me by the familiar spirit, and bring him up, whom I shall name unto thee.
I Samuel 28:8 (KJV)

And in the synagogue there was a man with a spirit of an unclean devil, and cried out with a loud voice, Saying, Let us alone; what have we to do with thee, thou Jesus of Nazareth? Art thou come to destroy us? I know thee who thou art; the Holy One of God. And Jesus rebuked him, saying, Hold thy peace, and come out him. And when the devil had thrown him in the midst, he came out of him, and hurt him not.
Luke 4: 33-35 (KJV)

This is probably one of the hardest chapters to write because this was the disaster that put me at my Father's feet. This made me realize God loves me and no matter how hard or deep I fall, His grace and mercy won't let me drown. God knows when someone is for real. He knows that because of all the things we go through, and then the things we have no control over, until we fully understand Him. We must accept Him for the loving parent He is and trust He has only good intentions for all His creations, His children, the adopted sons and daughters.

I've been procrastinating because the story of Thomas is sad. It's quite painful to see what the wiles of the devil can do. It makes my heart break to know that Thomas may be fulfilling his purpose. Like Judas, who was chosen by God, called by Jesus, to fulfill a purpose. He had to betray Christ. Sometimes, your purpose may not be so nice, but if it's in God's will, it'll be all right. Understand, I was chosen from the beginning, and someone had to be used to reveal satan's devices and put me at my Father's feet. Sometimes, you just have to see and experience it up close to know that it's real. I don't know, but I thank God, He took my life and adopted me as His child, but so is Thomas. Only, I don't know if anyone will ever discover all the curses that plague his life, or if he'll ever fully understand the truth, or will he literally die in the grips of satan.

I'm glad I received the revelation that when you die, you still can be changed. After all, you are a child of God, and no one can pluck you from His hands. Death for those who sleep, is just a time when our Father will cleanse you, just like Moses who couldn't take his anger into the Promise Land. Just like the body, how it replenishes itself while one sleeps, and Christ says you only sleep until He returns. So, as you can see, even though this was nothing nice, that agape love God puts in us prevails because I pray many blessings for Thomas. I pray fervently that he will be delivered and be able to live an abundant life in this life.

It all started when the devil made me doubt what I knew in

my heart to be true. I knew who had been chosen to be my husband, and he too had chose me, and made that fact known. The devil doesn't deserve all the blame. We usually aid in the devil's destructive behavior in our lives. I spoke it out of my mouth. I said, "God had to tell me who my husband was." I spoke it several times, to many people. Of course, the devil over heard this and chose to use it to destroy me. Yes, for a minute, I thought it was the devil that told me who my husband was. Who was he to choose a husband for a child of God, when his only motive is to destroy? satan knew I was cursed, plagued with a crazy sexual desire, and the need to be needed. Man, all that and the devil too. Then came Thomas.

A phone call, a telemarketer, selling doors. I don't even talk on the phone like that. I should have known from the carnal conversation, and the play on Christ, something was up. Some how, he aroused all the things I was so curious about. He seemed to know me, but doesn't the devil know us all. Then, he told me he was my husband, the man that's supposed to be in my life. Even though, I gave him the testimony about my true husband. Just like the serpent in the garden who spoke doubt into the hearts of Adam and Eve, and even thought he could tempt Jesus, before His ministry.

He placed doubt in my heart, and the seed was planted. Thomas told me he knew me. He said he had dreamed me and could describe me from head to toe, and he did. He described things, he shouldn't know. You know, that made me wonder. Curious wasn't the word for it. It stirred juices; after all, I was plagued with an unusual sexual desire. The devil truly is cunning, and he knows his handy work.

We're talking about the devil here. What he attempts to do, and what God will do to make his wrong right, his bad good, because the devil is only out to destroy. God protects His own, but sometimes the lessons are hard, especially when you can't seem to get it right. You just can't pass the test. No, that's not it. It's just the Potter continuously molding the clay into perfection. Some of the fine cracks are just a little harder to get to, to make it perfect. Sometimes you have to get real close to the fire, but my God won't let you get burned. You're His. You belong to Him.

I finally decided to meet Thomas after many long talks on the phone. It was a ministry, only it was tainted with unleashed desire. I hated what I saw when I first met him. He wasn't bad looking. He looked like Malcolm X, until he opened his mouth and "Voile" Donald Duck. He wasn't appealing to me in the least. I just took it that God had a work for me to do, and I went with the flow. God knows I'm His, but the devil knew my weaknesses, and used them against me. You're always attracted to that which is supposed to be in you. Always trying to fill that void that can only be filled by the Holy Spirit of God.

After an unscheduled duel in the word of God with Thomas, he immediately gave his life to Christ. Then, he seduced and sexed me like I'd never been sexed before. The seduction wasn't that difficult. Remember I was cursed. He was a gifted writer without a recognized purpose. He was quite "virgintile," an untouched love. He was a broken vessel, a broken vessel of God. You see, God is always trying to get us to the point where we trust Him and only Him. Thomas moved into my house. He was a border. He rented the room in the basement, criminal record and all. No job and short chance of getting one. The seed God planted in him was the only chance of him actually living in this life. I constantly fought a battle of lust, even though, I wasn't attracted to this man at all.

I watched him become obsessed over me, and the fatal attraction was on. He did everything he could to try and win me over. He was passionate and kind, but he wasn't a man. He was just fulfilling the role the devil had him playing. Why not? It was normal for him. He'd been playing under the same direction for 26 years. This time, he was seriously being used, and the devil was tearing him apart.

Thomas told everyone I was his wife. He constantly told people about how he dreamed me five years before while he was in prison. A prison in a prison. satan had imprisoned his mind, and man had his body. He told how I visited him every night those past five years. He spoke of how I comforted him for five years. The devil was plotting against me for a long time. He had Thomas. He had his mind. Unadulterated porno, all in his mind. Sex with me, a true child of God, one who would do whatever her Father told her, even love the unlovable. He had spent five years in prison without one visitor, but I came every night. He did things to me in his mind, you can only dream about, and he'd been dreaming for five years. He had never been loved, and never loved anyone. He didn't even love himself. Then came me with the love of Christ, all in his mind, and a crazy sexual desire. Curses.

He was really trying to convince everyone, I was his wife, but he couldn't convince me. He even tried to use the vision I had two years before. A vision of the man I am to marry sitting down with me, my Pastor and his wife for what seemed like premarital counseling. The devil told me, John wouldn't do that. It couldn't be him. He tried to use the fact that I didn't see the man's face, therefore, I really didn't know who he was. I only saw what he was wearing, which was a white shirt and black pants. Then, the devil said, John only wears T-shirts and turtle-necks. He was seriously using anything he could to truly make me doubt my spiritual wedding, and it was working. satan planted a seed of doubt, watered it, and it was definitely growing.

His persistence caused me to speak a big no-no in my life because of what Thomas called denial. I said, "God will have to roll a boulder over me, and tell me you (Thomas) was my husband before I'd ever hear or believe it." The boulder came. I heard it immediately, and I believed it. I took it for face value, forgetting the things of God are a mystery, only to be revealed. The boulder rolled over me, and the devil knew I needed to hear something from God. He knew I needed to fill that void, and the curse was functioning in full force.

Always remember, never forget, there's power in the tongue. The power of life and death. All God did was speak, and the world was created. So, watch what you confess with your mouth. Thomas' love, or what he thought was love made him beg. It even took him to the point of playing the "let me see if I can make you jealous game," but there was nothing to get jealous over. Thomas unquestionably was not the guy I wanted in my life. That is a really bad thought, if you compare Thomas to the man I spent the last fourteen years with. Thomas was faithful, loving, prime rib and passionate delight, but he was full of the devil, and my Holy Spirit wasn't having any parts of that. But, that crazy sexual desire, that dreaded curse was playing with my flesh, and wearing me down. Working on my flesh, all in my mind, after the first taste. I should have remembered the Word, resist the devil and he will flee from you. Once you take the cork out the bottle, it's really hard to get it back in. It's like a Lay's potato chip, you can't just eat one. Pure example and manifestation of that ole cliché, "Don't play with fire, cause you might get burnt."

I was truly in love with my true love, my real husband, the one God joined me to, my Adam. Our spirits had met. We knew each other. It was real, whether we were together or apart.

First came the suicide threat. He didn't actually do anything. He just checked into a hospital where he met another crazy individual. He thought she would make me jealous. Kumi, the castrated African whore. She was kinda cute; she had the double D breast Thomas liked, but she wasn't me. He had fell in love with me, five years in his mind, and he wasn't settling for a substitute. The devil wanted me and only me. He was on a mission.

Then, the games really began, but they didn't work. The threat was no longer a threat, but a serious attempt, alcohol and pills. Then the telephone calls to tell me he was going to kill himself. It really didn't matter to me, so, I did nothing to stop him. In fact, I didn't even think about it, until the next day when Minister Usher called me at work to tell me Thomas was in the hospital. He wanted me to call him.

Evidently, Cynthia, the one that spent five years in his head came to his rescue. Thomas' stepmother and his father swears I called them that night. That's why he didn't die. It wasn't me. I didn't call anyone. It had to be his guardian angel. It was the same one that came to him when he was in prison and stayed in his head for five years because I really didn't care.

Thomas constantly called me, but I wouldn't take his calls. Since I wouldn't take his calls, he wrote me from the hospital. He was a nuisance. He called everyone I knew, and hounded them about me. He just wouldn't quit, but the devil's plan didn't work, this time. I'm here to tell you, he'll never give up. He's on a mission. He can't win, but his job is to kill, steal, and destroy what God intends, which is for us to accomplish the purpose He sent us here for. Don't you know, the closer you get to your deliverance, who and what God wants you to be, the harder the devil works, and the more devious he gets. So, while Thomas was in the hospital, beginning his next journey to prison, I received my boulder. Another chapter, and another mark of the devil.

Thomas went back to prison, but he didn't stop trying to contact me. He continued to write. He continued to try to contact me through my friends and associates. He was determined. It wasn't until I had my devastating boulder experience, did I take the time to seriously commune with God about all that was going on. After all of this, and almost being killed, I knew God was on my side, and He was working on something. Then, it happened.

In the midst of my ex, Monroe and his girlfriend, Flora, in my kitchen, after a barbecue, I heard it. It was loud and clear. "Thomas is your husband." That's what I heard. Then, Flora spoke about how she knew Monroe was her husband. She said she dreamed him. That's when a spirit said, "See he dreamed you too. Thomas is your husband." Believing God was speaking to me, knowing I will do whatever God tells me, because He knows what's best for me, I accepted the fact that Thomas was my husband. After all, he was the only Thomas I knew. Two days later, Thomas called me from jail. I wrote him, but he never received the letters. The first letter he received was the one telling him what I had heard. The one that said, I was his wife, and if God said it, I had to believe it. That was a fact, but it wasn't the truth, and I was functioning in the integrity of my heart.

I wrote Thomas everyday. I ministered to him. We had a written ministry. It was great. I love being in God's Word especially when I have a designated purpose. My purpose was to groom a husband. During this time, Thomas started doing things that would help him survive, and take care of himself and a family when he got out. For the first time in his life, he appeared to have hope. Only the hope he had developed was all wrong. His hope was in me. I became Thomas' will to live, and his will to survive, even though, he said, it was God, but I knew better. If I wasn't in the conversation, neither was God. I told him, without God, we could have no relationship. I knew he really wasn't the man I wanted or desired. I also knew all things are possible through Christ Jesus, even finding love on a one-way street. Hosea did it, but I'm not Hosea. He was the man. Of course, the man chooses. I just agree, and I really didn't agree with Thomas, but again, all this was being done out of innocence and the integrity of my heart. Just can't stress that enough. God will not hold you accountable for some things you do wrong if they are done out of the integrity of your heart. Thank you Lord.

    I focused on making everything right for Thomas. I wanted the best for my man. I bought him a wardrobe of clothes, so he would be presentable to come into my world, and go into the work force. I bought him a realm of colognes. My man had to smell good. I managed to keep my car, so he would have something to drive. That is after he got his driver's license, for the first time in his life. He had many first times in his life with me. I sent him money to get the things he needed, as I prepared the life he was supposed to live. After all, I was used to role reversal, breaking the chain of command, ship out of order. Definitely not in line with God's Word, the man is supposed to be the man, taking care of the woman.

    Then, I had to do something I really didn't want to do. I had to mail a letter I wrote months before when the doubt truly set in, before Thomas played the suicide game. I had to let the man I claimed as my husband, know we couldn't have a relationship. I told him it wasn't in God's will. Maybe that was the problem, I made a claim that wasn't mine to make. I could choose, pray, and agree, but I had no right to claim, only God knows best. I mailed the letter hesitantly, but I did it. I waited anxiously for a response. I knew I wouldn't like the response I would receive because John had been through so much with me. He had finally let his guard down, only to have me do exactly what he said I would do. That's right, HE SAID IT. After our spiritual wedding, he said, I'd trample all over his feelings. Remember what you confess with your mouth. So, you just keep right on confessing things. I didn't do it on purpose, but I just knew it couldn't be in God's will, since I heard Thomas was my husband. I had to set him free, despite how much I loved him, and truly wanted to be with him.

Then came the day for Thomas to get out of prison. My son told me to immediately pray when Thomas got out. He said pray before I even thought about making a move. He said, it was easy to do God in jail. He should know, after all, he is Darrell, and his life has been full of turmoil. God gave me a revelation, "There's something in a name," and his real name means something. We prayed, but there was an urgency about being together that overruled the sincerity of the prayer and the seriousness of the situation. We both remembered the first time, how he sexed me, and how he made my knees tremble. We couldn't wait. We rushed home. After driving six hours, we got married. BIG TIP: If you're rushing and haven't truly heard from God, you better STOP. We didn't want to get caught in sin. It was wrong from the beginning. Everything, pointed to that, but I wasn't looking or paying attention, and Thomas really didn't care. That broken vessel, that abandoned child needed to be loved, and he had loved me for five years in his mind. The devil is so cruel. I was cursed with a desire that needed to be satisfied, but I wanted to satisfy it legally, within the rules of man. I really didn't want to sin. I truly believed exactly what I heard God speak to me, until the first night. The first night, after we said "I do," God stepped in and said, "No, you don't." Evangelist Belinda Moss, called them familiar spirits, and I was ready to chalk the whole detestable situation up to that. I made a defective choice based on what I heard. It wasn't a reflection of the truth about me. I wasn't going on a guilt trip. The truth be told, I heard what I heard, and that's a fact, but it wasn't the truth. The truth has to be revealed, and I took what I could see, that which the devil presented to me.

It wasn't doubt. It was just out right wrong. I began to detest Thomas, this man I called my husband. I tried though, because I still believed this Thomas was who God spoke to me about. It got worse every day. It's okay to take a break, but he began to take advantage of me. Thomas wasn't even trying, and I wasn't saying anything. I tried to let him be "The Man," but he sure wasn't acting like a man. I got tired of it. Evidently, so did God because he made it so we couldn't even come together to know one another. No sex for me, even the curse had no power. Thank you Lord for stepping in! Thank you for your anointing, that burden removing, yoke destroying power.

The devil must have seen God intervening because at that point, Thomas attempted to try to be the man, to be a husband. It was too late. I couldn't stand him. I couldn't stand the sight of him. I couldn't stand the smell of him. God put a stench on him I just couldn't stomach. I couldn't even sleep with him. I literally mean sleep. I couldn't even share a bed with him, that's how bad it was. He was making me physically sick. I hadn't been sick for at least eight years, and would never get sick. If I thought I was getting sick, I would bind that demon, lay hands on myself, rebuke the sickness, cast it out, and be healed in the Name of Jesus. I couldn't do it in this case. I lost my part-time job because I was sick. I couldn't function on my daily job because I was sick. I couldn't do anything. Thomas was literally sucking the life out of me, zapping my virtue.

I moved Thomas to the loft room; we couldn't share a room. Clothes and all. He would try to make me feel guilty by preaching the marriage scriptures to me. It was then I really realized we had only said "I do," but God said, "No, you don't." He made it clear, He didn't join us together. What we had was not a marriage. God wouldn't even allow us to come together. You know when God makes you one.

That's when the tricks of the devil started to prevail, and God allowed me to see I was out of place. He never called me to be Thomas' wife. I was only his guardian angel, his mentor, discipling him to seek deliverance. He revealed to me that Thomas had made a pact. Pacts can only be made by the devil. Thomas had vowed, he would never come out of prison unless he could have me. Remember, the devil heard what I spoke aloud with my mouth. He knew about the curse that prevailed in my life. So, he utilized my curse, my confessions, and Thomas' pact to try and take me out, and keep Thomas from being delivered.

Then, my work really began. God began to feed me every day. Then, everyday or night, I ended up ministering to Thomas that which God had given me. Thomas would keep me up every night until 3 or 4 o'clock in the morning. He cried and begged, and cried and begged, and cried and begged. Thank God, during at least two of those long grueling hours, his spirit seemed to absorb what God had for him. He would finally go to bed, which was now back in the basement. But, he wouldn't rest. He would phone me from downstairs to talk, knowing I had to go to work. Work which was preceded by morning devotions at 0415 hours and physical training every morning at 0530 hours.

He was hard pressed on this marriage thing, but there was no marriage. God had not joined us together. There was no love on my behalf, and what Thomas had for me was not love. It was an obsession, a fatal attraction. He made me his idol, a god. Thomas didn't mind living in the basement. He didn't mind not being with me as long as he could talk to me. That's sick, and he was sickening. I really mean sickening, to the point of regurgitating. It was sickening to go downstairs. First, I had to get pass the filth, and then that retched smell. I also had to get pass seeing a grown man, balled up in a knot, on the sofa, crying like as baby. Every day. It was utterly disgusting and depressing, and those spirits had crept into my house. There was no peace. There was no solace. There was only depression.

God wouldn't allow me to talk to anyone about what was going on in my life except one of my soldiers. At times, I thought I was going crazy. I know this is all spiritual, and that was the only way I had to see it. God was seriously at work here. First, I thought it was just for Thomas, but as I look closer, I can see it was for me too.

I ministered to Thomas every day until the very essence of life almost left my body. Then, God gave me a break. We finally reached a plateau. It was the "Lazarus come forth" stage. Thomas finally realized who I was to be in his life, and what God had in store for him. He had to go through, and I couldn't take him any further. He needed professional help. Thomas and I prayed that night. He cried on my shoulder. That was the first and the last time he was, willingly on my behalf, in my arms. That night Thomas calmly left my room. We both went to sleep in our separate areas. There was no calls, but we had made plans to go to church together the next day.

That next morning, I woke up with just the intention of going to church, but God had other plans. The Lord had me anoint my house, and everything in it. He told me to bind and cast out all the demon spirits that had crept into the house during the Thomas tenure. He told me to anoint every opening in the house, and open the front door and ensure all the demons went out that way. I was obedient, and did just that. I anointed, and laid hands on everyone in the house, including Thomas, who had told me never to lay hands on him again. I prayed like God told me. Then, I went back to my room where God sent me into a crazy praise and diverse prayers. He had me pray for the wounded child, the child within, the children of abuse. I was shouting up a storm, and the presence of the Lord was heavy in my room. After God got finished shouting me, He sat me at His feet and I worshipped Him. Then, the phone rang. Guess who? Thomas.

Of course, it was Thomas. The devil was still busy. He decided he wasn't going to church with us, but he wanted to talk. No, I didn't have time for that or any of his nonsense. I knew God had a blessing for me, and no devil in hell was going to stop me from getting my blessing. Then, more obstacles, the trash needed to go out, and it was beginning to snow. Everything was trying to keep me from going to church, but I knew there was a blessing waiting for me and I was going to get it. So I left.

When I got to church, I was asked to greet at the door. It had been a long time since I had done that. Suddenly, there was a change in the agenda. Someone forgot to put the Creed into the program, so the Chaplain decided to have a church altar prayer. God had him pray for the " wounded child, the child within." Mind you, there was no children in the congregation. It was second Sunday, which is children's church Sunday, and all the children are at another location. God definitely was on one accord, and confirming His will.

Then came the Rhema, the spoken Word of God. The Word was on Lazarus being called forth, called from the grave by Jesus, and ultimately having to take off his grave clothes. That day, God gave me closure on the whole Thomas issue. He told me, it was time for Thomas to stand on his own two feet. I had to let go. He made it all too clear. You see the devil meant it for evil, but God was going to use it for good. The devil thought he would trap us both, Thomas and I, in something God had nothing to do with, and we would ultimately be doomed. But God. But God, Yes God, took this situation to be glorified in. It was time for Him to deliver a person who had been broken from childhood and another who was faithful, but still needed to be delivered from curses and come to the full knowledge of the truth.

God finally revealed the whole situation. I could talk about it, and I did. It was a testimony to reveal the radical actions of God. You can't box Him in. There was still one thing that kept creeping up in my mind. That was, why did I have to marry him? Why did it have to be legal? God even answered that question. Thomas needed extensive medical and psychological help. What he was about to endure would be work, very traumatic work, and it would be expensive. Not very many people come back from where he had to go to be delivered and set free, but my medical benefits would afford him the moneys needed for the treatment required, and I wouldn't be burdened.

When I got home that Sunday, Thomas was downstairs on the telephone, as usual. He's a phone-a-holic. The children had choir rehearsal that day. So, they changed their clothes and left. Although, I'm usually not a nosey person, that day something told me to listen in on his conversation. I heard Thomas tell his sister I argued with him constantly, day and night. He was standing by the TV, so she could hear all the noise. She thought it was me. He was really belittling me. Then, she told him, no man should have to live with such a contentious woman. She told him, if he came there to live with her, he would have to go to church every Sunday. He said, he didn't do that. So, his not going to church with us was no mistake. He had managed not to go to church for over a month. I should have known the devil didn't want him to chance going to church and being set free.

When I got tired of listening to him lie and put me down, I went downstairs to let Thomas know I was home. I told him Minister Sweeney said hello. I really wanted his sister to hear that all that noise wasn't me because I never even talked to Thomas except during our late night ministries, and I didn't want to talk then. It was always in the middle of the night when God wouldn't allow me to go to sleep. Thomas hurried to get off the phone. Then he followed me upstairs. He told me he was leaving Friday. He said until then don't speak to him. He said he didn't want anyone in the house to talk to him. I had no problem with that. In fact, it was a relief. I didn't want to talk to him anyway.

Then Richard called. Thomas came back upstairs. He wanted to talk, but I ignored him. He did say, don't talk to him. When I wouldn't talk to him, he came in my room. I pointed at the door to get him to leave. He said he wasn't a dog to be pointed out, but I was determined I wasn't going to speak to him. Then, he went into my bathroom and started taking pills out of my medicine cabinet. Here we go again, I thought to myself. I told him the pills he was taking wouldn't kill him. I put him in God's hands. It was his choice. Then, I said," If you want to play this game, then take the pills that will kill you." He kept saying he wasn't playing a game, and grabbed the pills from the other side of the medicine cabinet. I really didn't take him serious, until he dumped the whole bottle of Prozac down his throat, thirty pills, one gulp. I told Richard what was going on. We immediately began to pray. Then, when I saw Thomas pick up another bottle of pills, I told Richard, "I'm leaving, I'm not going to stay here while he kills himself." I handed Thomas the phone and Richard tried to talk to him. I left.

I drove to the neighborhood Safeway parking lot, where I cried out to God. What was I going to do? God told me to go back to the house, and call the paramedics. He told me that it wasn't my fault. The suicide demon came through the phone when Thomas was talking to his sister. It was all in the plan because Thomas needed to go to the hospital. He needed to be an inpatient, to get treatment. He had to be protected from himself, and all the demons in his head. So, I gathered myself together, and went back to the house.

Thomas was on the phone as usual, but he dropped the phone when he saw me calling the rescue squad on the second phone line. He snatched the phone off the wall, but he laid the cordless phone down on the kitchen table. I picked up the cordless phone, and called 911. At that point, he ran. The police came. I gave them a description of him, and the search was on.

They found him. You know, he didn't get far. It's really bad to say, but I had really hoped they wouldn't find him. He would have fallen asleep somewhere, and died in peace. I knew the journey he had to undergo, and it wasn't going to be an easy one. At least, he gave his life to Christ. So, he would only sleep, and be cleansed in the process until Christ's return. I guess the work God has for him is too valuable for anyone else to do.

They brought him back to the house. He denied taking anything, even though, there was empty pill bottles all over the house. Then, I found a suicide note, which meant I could go to the Magistrates office and get custody of him, so he could get treatment. It didn't come to that. The medications Thomas took were many, and very potent. Within ten minutes of him being back at the house, he started fading in and out. So, they strapped him to a gurney, and took him away.

I waited and went to the hospital about two hours after they left. I didn't want to see them put down the tube they used to pump his stomach. I didn't want to watch them pour charcoal into his gut, then watch it come back up. Even though, I'm a nurse, I really didn't want to do this one. When I did get there, it was pitiful. He was pitiful. Both nostrils full of blood, continuous retching to vomit up the thick black charcoal only to have them dump more down the tube. Thomas' suicide attempt this time consisted of 30 Prozac, 50 Robaxin 500mg, 50 Benadryl 50 mg, 5 Percocet, 20 Naprosyn, and 10 pills of some drug the child my daughter baby-sits takes for ADHD. They said he had a lot of pills in his system, but they got most of them still intact.

Thomas was transferred to the nearest military medical center that morning. It's been all down hill since then. He spent two weeks at the medical center. He threatened the doctors, assaulted the patients, and was a nuisance to me. It was during this time I found out he had been throwing away my mail. What gave him the right? Thomas chose to leave WRAMC. He claimed he was going to live with his sister in another state. I'd get calls saying he was leaving. Only the next day, I would get a call from the University Hospital stating he was there. Apparently, another attempted suicide, but the hospital had no records, no history, no anything on him, and they wanted me to give them some information.

I eventually spoke to Thomas' doctors, even though, he forbade them to speak to me. With no history, after two weeks, the doctors decided Thomas should go to a mental institution. They sent him to a government, state operated mental institution, lots of crazy people, many demons. This was the beginning of a nightmare. Thomas couldn't convince me to be with him, and he was convinced I had him committed. Therefore, he chose to team up with Damon, my boulder.

Thomas called my Commander and First Sergeant. He demanded I be arrested. They told him, they'd look into the situation, but right now, all he could get was a little bit of money. Of course, he demanded that. Only later, he called back to tell my Commander he rescinded everything he said. He gave her some mental diagnosis, and admitted to her, I married him without knowing he had a mental history.

I started receiving threatening phone calls from Thomas. He would call me and others and say, he was going to kill me and my children. He said he took an offer from Damon for $11,000 to kill the children and I. Of course, that can't be proven, and Damon would only say Thomas was crazy, after all, he was locked up in a mental institution. I knew they were corresponding because the calls from Damon had started up again. God, this whole story is a nightmare. Thomas had everyone thinking I was really bad, even though, he knew better. If I told him he could come back into my life, right now, he would jump at the chance and break his neck doing it.

I called the mental institution to report the threatening

phone calls. I even called to let them know that he was threatening himself. The threats resulted in a competency and commitment hearing scheduled. A hearing that never took place. There was a meeting held on Thomas' behalf. He tried to make me look like I was crazy. Thomas' family, his doctors and myself sat to determine what would be best for him. At the conclusion of the meeting, Thomas' sister said she would take him home with her, if he didn't have to stay at the mental institution any longer. It was agreed that he would be released if he left the area and his sister would be awarded custody of him. So, he was finally going to leave after being there for almost two months. Lord help us all.

Thomas finally left the hospital. At first, he just went to his daddy's house right there in the city, where he harassed me. He called me constantly, but I wouldn't return any of his calls, or accept any of the long distance charges. He couldn't call me at work, at least not at my number because the Military Police had been notified and my phones were wired. Finally, he went to be with his mother and his sister, which is where God wanted him to be. Thomas had to go meet his demons head on. After a couple of days, I started getting weird pager messages and collect phone calls from Thomas. Then he would leave messages on my beeper, 771 (ILL backwards) and 666 (the mark of the devil).

When I finally talked to Thomas, he was threatening to kill his mother. He said he couldn't take it. He said his mother kept telling him she loved him and the past was the past. During our written ministry while Thomas was in prison, he said he had forgiven his mother, but he really hadn't. As I ministered to him, all his demons started coming forth. I bound and cast out several of them. First the suicide demon, then the homicide demon, then guilt, until I remembered, before Thomas left he had a legion of demons. So, I bound the legion and cast them out. Then even more demons came up. I listened to them tell how it was too late for Thomas. They said they had him too long. They spoke of how they were going to kill him and his mother too, or maybe just kill his mother, and leave Thomas to be tormented in prison for the rest of his life. At least then he wouldn't be doing any work for God. He would be trapped in his own prison in his mind. They continued to speak. There was so many of them, each talking and taking turns to speak. Yes, there was different ones, all with their own unique voice and personality. I couldn't listen anymore. I had to hang up. I hung up, and prayed for Thomas. I prayed God would help him take control of his life. There was no call back. That was my confirmation that it wasn't Thomas just acting out. He had adopted the demons that plagued his whole family. I prayed for him, but that's all I could do.

A couple of days later, I received another phone call from Thomas telling me he had to leave. He said his mother was in the hospital. She was in a mental institution. She had lost her mind. She couldn't stand him being there. That's the power and weight of guilt. I guess she couldn't. I wouldn't be able to either, if I had abandoned my eight year old child.

To hear Thomas tell it, his mother just up and left. She didn't say anything. She didn't say where she was going, only to have her child come home to a "For Sale" sign on the house. Then all through his adolescent years, whenever, he could find her, she would say she didn't want him and have him put in yet another foster home or institution. He ends up in jail, second-degree rape. Was he looking for love? Then, prison, after trying to rob a bank, by blowing up the ATM machine, how stupid. Five more years of isolation. Then, Thomas tried to kill himself only to be sent back to prison for parole violation. Again, the suicide attempts, not once but may times, running up medical bills, only to end up in a mental institution. Thomas had turned out to be exactly like his mother, who can physically walk, but has chose to be in a wheel chair for over 27 years, a self made invalid. People imprisoned in their own minds, trapped by the devil, unbroken curses. Recognize the devices of satan and his demonic forces which are very real, even in this life.

God has revealed to me, the message of Ismael and Isaac. Right here is this twisted picture of the pangs of satan. You need to know the devil will always try to keep you from your true blessing. He will always present a counterfeit before the real blessing God has in store for you. Unlike Sarah and myself, we must truly trust God. When we have heard from God, we must accept it and be patient and know that God is God and what He says is true. We must look beyond what we can see with our senses in the natural, the facts of the matter. We must seek God and seek the truth in the spiritual realm, just believe, and never doubt Him. We must trust God that He is not slack at fulfilling His promises, and that which He started in us He is able and will complete.

You see, the truth is God said what He said, "Thomas is your husband." Remember the names have been changed, but in real life Thomas is my husband, only it wasn't this broken vessel. God told me, there was something in a name, a while before I even said "I Do" to this Thomas. It wasn't until I wrote this book and researched the names, did I realize the name of my Adam means the name God told me was my husband, and there are no coincidences in God. We must seek the mysteries of God's will, the hidden treasures in secret places. His perfect will for our lives.

CHAPTER EIGHT

THE BOULDER

See to it that no one takes you captive through hollow and deceptive philosophy, which depends on human tradition and the basic principles of this world rather than on Christ.
Colossians 2:8 (NIV)

But wicked men and impostors will go from bad to worse, deceiving and leading astray others and being deceived and laid astray themselves. But as for you, continue to hold onto the things that you have learned and of which you are convinced, knowing from whom you learned (them).
2 Timothy 3:13,14 (AMP)

I can't say it enough, we must watch what we say with our mouth. God's Word is true. He said, the power of death and life is in the tongue. Look what it's done to the lives of our children and even ourselves. But, confessing or speaking truly began to mean something to me when my boulder came. It was all too clear. It was definitely a boulder. My boulder, the one I spoke out of my mouth. The very words the devil heard. He hears everything we say. You see, a boulder comes down on whatever is in it's path, and then it crashes. Damon was my boulder. He really tried to smash me, but God, my Lord and Savior saved me. I mean that literally, saved me. He saved my physical life.

God is God. He said, "No weapon formed against me shall prosper..." No, not one. I thank God, His Word is true. He said, the battle is not mine, but His and when it came time, He fought it for me. God literally saved my life from someone, the devil, who tried to kill me.

Thomas was in the hospital; the hospital stay prior to him going back to prison. I was glad he was safe, I was also glad he was gone. He continued to call. He kept calling, he wouldn't stop. I focused on God. I felt guilty about loosing control of my flesh. At least, it was good, to the flesh, that is, but I still felt guilty. I was confused, and the only place I could turn was to God.

God blessed me with a nice home, and I anointed and dedicated my home to Him. It was for His use. Then, I met Damon. He was sitting outside the Chaplain's office the first time I saw him from afar. He seemed distraught and my heart went out to him, but I didn't say anything to him. Don't you know, the devil knows the necessity of your physical nature.

Then, we actually met, this time in the Chaplain's office. We started talking. He was a mechanic. Wouldn't you know I needed a mechanic right then. He told me what was wrong with my Spirit. That's the car God gave me when I was stranded in Germany, after totaling my VW Jetta in a 360 degree crash on the autobahn. His conversation was so fluent and nice as he fed me a story that made me see potential. Something I've never really looked for in a man. My sister, Sabrina, always said, I deserved much more that I usually settled for. I had never been with a man who had money, or even professed to have money and seemed to want to show it. In other words, his gift of gab and deceit captivated me.

I loaned him my car that first day, and he brought it back. The conversation continued. He told me about the various things that weren't right in his life, at that time. He was staying with one of the deacons of the church, but the deacon was having company from out of town, and he needed a place to stay. He had just got out of jail. He said, he had been falsely arrested, and was suing the county police. He said he was looking at getting a good settlement, at least $750,000. I continued to listen, and the devil had all the foothold he needed. He had gained my attention. You must be careful what you receive in your spirit, even through what seems to be casual conversation. Know that all words are effective to bring about some form of change.

My heart went out to him. I'm sure that's the reason God continues to bless me. It's that heart of mine, a true heart of compassion. I enjoyed his conversation, so I invited him over. That night turned to day. White shirt, black pants, educated, money coming, drummer in the church, was this the answer? I had been made to doubt who my true husband, my Adam is, and another who fit the bill appeared. Then, that crazy lust arose. Where did it keep coming from? Why couldn't I control that desire that was in me? I didn't understand it. I truly loved the Lord. I knew it was a sin against the body, the body that is the temple of God, but I couldn't help myself.

So, as you might have already figured out, I attempted to have sex with him. Thank God, it didn't work. He was a Superman. That's the medical term, in nursing terminology. It describes someone who has an extra gene for their gender, an extra sex gene, a XYY, not normal. But, it's more than that, a superman is usually a sexual deviate with a criminal mind and tendencies, very violent. Needless to say, what I'm telling you now, I learned later in nursing school.

Damon was very handy. The devil knew I could use a handy man around the house. I figured I would be able to get my car worked on, for free, and it seemed like a good deal, and a good idea. Don't you know, there's nothing free, but salvation. Even that's not free, it'll cost you your life, but you'll get it back. So, I allowed him to stay in my house. After all, I did tell God, I would house the homeless. Only, I don't remember consulting God on this one. Somehow, Damon moved from the family room to my bedroom. He didn't ask, and I didn't invite him. It wasn't like we had a relationship or anything. That's when he began to take control of my life, and tell me how to handle my business. Then, he took control of my house, my finances, then my children. He took control of my whole life, and I allowed it. I seemed to have no control. I just relinquished all control to him. I really don't know why because I didn't want to.

Despite, him having control, my spirit wouldn't mesh with his. I didn't even like him. He was so conceded. All he did was talk about himself, and all these things he said he had done, only there was no fruit. None that I could see. He talked about how he played with star bands, owned auto shops, and raced cars. He went on and on and on. I could see him becoming very fruitful, only it was my assets he was using.

He started making propositions and saying how he could do this and do that to make money. He seemed to be able to do it, so I loaned him the money. Yes, I loaned him the money. Even though, until this very day, he denies it. What does a single parent with four children look like giving a man thousands of dollars. Get real.

First, it was a couple of hundred, then it was thousands. He was working deals, used cars was the first scam. He even looked the part. You know he had to hook himself up, the best tennis shoes, clothes, musical equipment, vehicles, etc. He had me setting the house up the way he thought it should be. New dishes, another vacuum cleaner, hose at the sink. He even started building a room out of the loft area. He rewired the telephones to make them work when and where he wanted them too. Little did I know, he was setting my home up for himself. Can we say, con artist?

I didn't like him at all, but I couldn't let him walk away with my money. He belittled my children. He said Ebony was a whore, and Ashley was a dike. He belittled me by treating me like I didn't know how to handle my business, but look who had the house. He always talked about other people. He was always putting everyone down and making up lies about them. He was a big liar. He even told mega lies about my Pastor. He criticized and lied on just about everyone in the church. To hear him tell it, every woman in the choir tried to sleep with him. He could really tell some stories. Really unbelievable. Sometimes I think he believed them, but he carried his baggage with him, literally. That's how I finally knew the whole truth. I was being set up by the devil. He was out to get me, again. This had to be my boulder because it was seriously weighing down on me, and pressing me from all directions.

Damon had taken me for almost $12,000, at that time. It was like a poker game, he had taken my money and I was all in. He was telling people we had a relationship, at least those he wanted to think that. He would talk about me like a dog to everyone else while he tried to plot on them. He was playing a game, and I was just holding out as long as I could for my money. For a while, I really thought he might be my deliverance. Don't you know, only God can deliver you from the toils of this life.

I brought who I now considered to be satan, in a rare form, into my house. I put my children in danger. They decided it was him or them. As much as they hated going to their daddy's house, they broke their necks to get there that summer, even though Damon made it seem like they had to go. I had my oldest son get to the point of rage, he wanted to kill Damon. Most of all, I started turning my back on the church, meaning I was no longer fellowshipping with the saints to gain strength, as a normal function. I was being pulled out, and I couldn't do anything about it. He was setting me up to be isolated and alone. Then, the devil was going to attempt to take me out. Oh, but he must have forgot who my Father is. Maybe he thought I was phony because I had this sexual desire he couldn't seem to arouse, but he knew was there. That's the devil for you. I told you he knows your weaknesses, and his handy work.

After managing to be almost $18,000 in the hole, that is after being debt free for almost two months. Long time, huh? Kids gone, 4x4 Jeep Grand Cherokee, CD collection, and another room in the house started, I guess the devil said it was time. I don't know what happened, but the winds were raging, and the war had begun.

It was in July, and I was supposed to pick my sister and her family up from the airport. I went to work that day, nothing really special at work. Damon called and inquired about my sister coming into town. He said, he wouldn't pick them up from the airport. That wasn't a problem. I never asked or expected him too. That night, I decided to stop at the store to get some things my sister needed for her children. I was a little late getting home. You would have thought the stock market crashed the way the tempers were stirring. I wasn't concerned, after all, I was the one who had to make the trip to airport. I knew how long it would take me, and if I was a little late, my sister would be okay.

My thought process evidently wasn't on the right wave length because Damon was really in a rage. He yelled at me. He was really angry, and started to take off in the Jeep. He said, he was going to get my sister because I was late, and no one knew where I was. I stopped my motion and said, "No, I'm going." I had to rush to get back in the vehicle. The big black bag, I usually carry with all my necessary items in it, which I intended to carry, was rudely thrown out of the vehicle by Damon. He said we would need all the space we could get, even though, he failed to get the two car seats he promised to get.

We left in a hurry. He drove like a maniac, not like he didn't always drive like an idiot. He always thought he was racing. Did I tell you, he professed to be a professional race car driver. Most of the things he said he did or was appeared to be real. That's what I really don't understand. He had so much going on for himself, but he chose to be used by the devil, to gain the things of this world. You know, you will receive the reward of the god you serve. He was proficient at many things. He even said he had a Master's Degree in Mechanical Engineering. I haven't proven that to be untrue, yet. Sometimes, I think what a waste, he is a vessel God can use, but he chooses to serve the devil.

Now that I think about it, God was setting me up. This particular statement offends many people because no one wants to think Our Father would do that, but someone has to go through and then live to testify, to minister what He wants us to know. At this moment God wants us to know there definitely is the power of life and death in our tongue. Your words are life. God may not actually do the dastardly deeds, but He absolutely allows it. You should check out Job. Yes, He was setting me up.

I've dealt with every type of man and demon, but God still prevails. Damon was full of demons. He embraced his demons. He served them, and they served him back. Only, he kept his demons under his control.

Anyway, while we were traveling to get my sister. Damon continued to verbally rage in anger. I wasn't saying anything, in fact, I didn't even acknowledge him. I was tired, and he was sickening. He talked about me, my children, my house, my cars, my job, my body, the males I associated with, and the people in the church. He just went on and on and on. He kept ranting and raving until I couldn't take it anymore. After crossing over the state line, I said, "Would you please shut up!" Then, he immediately sped up and crossed over the state line where he slammed on brakes, in the inside traffic lane, on this busy interstate. He just stopped. Completely stopped, right in the middle of traffic. I don't know how we didn't get rear ended. Yes, I do. It was God, My Father, who is always there, Jehovah Shammar, Himself.

He continued to drive straight across the road, all four lanes in one maneuver. Then, he pulled onto the side of the road. He really blew up and continued to yell at me. He threatened to kill me. He put his hand around my throat. He said he could kill me with one squeeze of his hand, then he commenced to squeezing. I was really tired of being tormented by him. So, I told him. "Fine! Kill me, just do it. My soul is all right with God, and my kids will be well taken care of." I did nothing to stop him. Then, he stopped and jumped out of the Jeep. I attempted to get behind the steering wheel and drive off, but it didn't work. We had a struggle over the keys that were still in the ignition. I must say the man was stronger, but didn't God make him that way. Then, Damon really got enraged. He grabbed me by my arm and threw me out onto Interstate 95 North. I landed in the far right lane. He came and scooped me up out of the road. He kept saying, I pushed him to do that. My hands and knees were skinned up. I ran, but he caught me. He threw me into a gravel gutter. That's when I started calling out to Jesus. I cried out to God. I mean, I really cried, and that's something very hard for me to do. He kept yelling at me to get up. I wouldn't. He started pulling me by my hair to get me in the Jeep. I wasn't going anywhere. I wasn't going to get in a vehicle for him to kill me.

He finally managed to get me up by the Jeep. We fought. He put an elbow hold on me that wouldn't quit. That's probably when I scratched his arm because he showed the police some minor scratches when they finally showed up. He did finally get me in the vehicle as we continued to struggle. Then, a man in a white truck pulled up, and some how I managed to get to his truck. His door was locked, as I stood there bamming on his window. I was struggling to get in, while Damon was choking me from behind. The man pulled off, and again, I was left alone with him. I ran into the street myself, this time. I figured, if I was going to die, I might as well do it myself. I couldn't. So, I tried to stay as far away from him as possible. He managed to get my purse, and he did something under the hood of the Jeep. He disabled the vehicle. Again, somehow, he caught me, and threw me out onto Interstate 95. This time I landed in the center lane. My glasses got smashed, but I remember seeing an eighteen wheeler coming directly at me, less than a hundred feet, traveling at least 55 miles per hour. I don't know how I got out the road. It wasn't Damon this time, for sure. I was still living, and I was armed in my spirit. Damon and I had words. God made Himself clear. He started to speak through me. He told the devil, this is a war between satan and God and he, satan couldn't win because he was already a loser. Then, immediately the police came. Damon ran on the passenger side of the Jeep, where he threw my wallet in bushes, in the dark.

Then, Damon ran to the police. He told them I assaulted him, and showed them the minor scratches on his arm. They checked both of us out, but they hand cuffed him and put him in the police car. I needed to find my wallet, all my identification was in it. The police officer wouldn't look for my wallet because the bushes were full of Poison Oak. She wouldn't give me the flashlight either because it could be used as a weapon. I was determined to find my wallet. The search was on, with or without a light. I searched for about ten minutes before I remembered God was able to do all things. So, I cried out to God, and He heard my cry. He told me to go about 6 feet to the right of where I was standing in the dark and bend down. Note, it was approximately 12 a.m. midnight, there were no lights on the road, I had no glasses, the bushes were high and full of Poison Oak. Many obstacles. But, glory be to God, I reached down and put my hand right on my wallet. All I could do was cry and shout, "Thank you Lord!" I came out the bushes praising God and thanking Him for the victory. The story was unreal, but isn't that like God. It was a testimony and I shared it with the police officer who waited with me while the tow truck came to tow the Jeep away. Then she took me to the police station.

I was only taken to the police station because the Jeep wouldn't start, and to make a statement and press charges against Damon. I answered a lot of questions. That's when I found out Damon had a very long and extensive criminal record. One of his charges was murder. They took pictures of my injuries. I was really scraped and battered. Even, the choke ring around my throat was visible to the naked eye. While I was making my statement, Damon was in the back of the jail demanding his phone call. When he got it, he called my boss. It was very late, but she was concerned for my safety. She said she would be there for me, but not for him, even though they had a used vehicle transaction pending.

All the police officers started coming out to where I was, telling me I shouldn't let this go unpunished. They kept saying how sick he was. One officer said he was mentally deranged, a pathological liar. They all said he was a fast talking liar. He hadn't been there ten minutes, and they already knew him. I kept wondering, was I stupid or what? The devil sure had it out for me, but God said hold your peace, I'll fight your battle.

I kept trying to call home. Someone still needed to pick my sister and her family up from the airport. No one would answer the phone. I found out later, Damon set the phones so no one would be able to hear them ring. After what seemed like hours, my son finally answered the phone. He said, he thought it was strange the phone hadn't rang all night. He noticed the caller ID button was frantically flashing, which meant there was numerous calls registered on the box. He said he checked the box, and there was numerous calls from an out of state pay phone. The pay phone was the phone at the police station where I was calling from.

Before I finally contacted Kenny, I eventually called my other sister, Rayna, to see if she could make arrangements to get Sabrina picked up, and get in touch with my family. I didn't have any phone numbers because Damon threw my black bag out the Jeep before we left. Sounds like a plot to me.

Kenny came and picked me up with Sherry. Sherry was Damon's little 17 year old female friend, who Kenny was trying to get with. I later found out, they, Damon and Sherry were plotting on me and whatever money they thought I might have or be able to acquire. They really didn't care how they got it, just as long as they got it. She told how Damon was telling everyone my house and vehicles belonged to him. He was telling everyone all the money he was spending was from his lawsuit. NO, oh No! It was ALL from me, every last nickel. She told us Damon asked her to marry him. She was spilling her guts. She had been used, but so had I. He had everyone fooled.

I immediately went and got an emergency restraining order against him. Then, we went home. We got home about four in the morning. Day had broke. My sister was already at the house, and she was mad. She remained angry until I told her what happened. Then, the hunt was on for whatever information would tell me about this man that came into my house and took control of my world, the devil.

We finally found his coveted brief case. He hid it in the trunk of the car, the illustrious 1988 Cougar, no less. He had jimmed the lock on the trunk, so it wouldn't open. Therefore, we had to climb through the back seat to get it open. All the answers were in the briefcase. Criminal, that was a very mild statement for what Damon was. Discharged U.S. Army delinquent, wife abuser, rapist, credit card thief, and murderer. He was not your run of the mill con artist, and I was caught up in something I really didn't know how to handle.

There was no love lost. My only though was the money. I had given of myself, and been taken by a professional con artist. Was I stupid? No, I was cursed. I knew I told God I wanted a husband. I knew He would give me one who would be able to take care of me and love me. I knew it wasn't Damon. He was sinister, and I really hated everything about him. I didn't like anyone having control of my life especially when it involved my children. He literally turned my children against me because I allowed him to continue in his sinister plan.

For those that don't believe the devil is real, and he can and will target you for his kill. You are sadly mistaken. Damon played the I love you game, but there was nothing there, not even sex. The only thing that kept me in the game was money, my money, or what I thought was my money. I realize now, I have no money, even that which I earn, is not mine, it belongs to God. He only allows me to earn it, and He allows me to have 90%, what I need to survive and prosper in this world. Without realizing it, I had put out almost $19,000 dollars. Where did it come from, especially for an individual I didn't even like. The devil sure is devious, and I felt like a sucker. That was my senses speaking to me, a total lie, because the truth is what God says about me, and He says I am more than a conqueror.

But God. Again, I say, but God, because He saw me through. God won't allow anything to happen to His children He doesn't allow. I know now God will deliver me from anything satan has devised against me. He will win because He is God, and in Him all things are possible, and all things come together for the good of those who love God and are called according to His purpose.

For a while fear set in. After all, this man tried to kill me. I really didn't know God the way I know Him now. Fear gripped me, and I was doing anything to survive. I changed all the locks on the doors, changed the security codes. I took out restraining orders. Pleaded the Blood of Jesus over me and my house, I even marked my house with the blood. I did anything, and everything. I was actually scared of Damon, even though, God saved me from him on Interstate 95 and declared I am His, and tells me He didn't give me the spirit of fear, but of a sound mind.

The devil even tried to take me out on my job. Damon brought false charges against me. He accused me of Solicitation to Commit Murder. I had to endure grueling hours of polygraph tests, questioning and sworn statements. He said, I asked him to kill Monroe. He claimed I was trying to collect on the insurance policy I have on him. Yeah, right. I was able to be conned for almost $19,000 cash money without an insurance policy, so why would I need to have Monroe killed.

Damon went so far as to try and convince Monroe I was out to kill him. He had Monroe convinced for a minute, and he conspired with Damon for a while, until Monroe realized he was being used. One time, I can say thank God for the curse because the "Miller Effect" kicked in. Damon thought Monroe's anger with me about possibly having another man would override the love he still had for me. I guess it goes to show you love does conquer all, just like Jesus' love for us because Monroe was right there for me. He used the excuse that he was protecting his girls, but God knows he was still trying to get with me.

Damon told so many lies on me. He was really trying to get even with me for him being arrested and the possibility he might go to jail again. I found out he was on parole, but he was still out on the streets, which meant I had no peace. We never seemed to meet in court. He always managed to get the date changed, but I was determined to see him in jail. After all he took me through and took me for. He almost cost me my life, my physical life, that is. I wasn't seeking revenge, only justice under the law, and we know all sinners are judged by the law.

Damon was a fast talking, sinister, demon possessed individual who had no power. He is a loser. He knows who I am, and who lives in me. Damon knew he had demons ruling his life, only he controlled his demons. His control was in total submission to the devil's will, only to receive the devil's reward. There was no end, still no closure, but the Lord is holding His ground. The battle isn't over yet, God did say, vengeance was His. I thank God for handling my business. I know now the devil can't win. I know now that I must watch the very words that precede from my mouth, for they are life or death to me and mine. Thank you Lord!

CHAPTER NINE

UNCONDITIONAL FORGIVENESS

And we earnestly beseech you brethren, admonish (warn and seriously advise) those that are out of line - the loafers, the disorderly and the unruly; encourage the timid and fainthearted, help and give your support to the weak souls (and) be very patient with everybody - always keeping your temper. See that none of you repays another with evil for evil, but always aim to show kindness and seek to do good to one another and everybody.
1 Thessalonians 5: 14,15 (AMP)

If we (freely) admit that we have sinned and confess our sins, He is faithful and just (true to His own nature and promises) and will forgive our sins (dismiss our forgiveness) and continuously cleanse us from all unrighteousness - everything not in conformity to His will in purpose, thought and action.
1 John 1:9 (AMP)

You know this chapter really has nothing to do with the curse, but then again, it does. Yes, it really does. It definitely has something to do with the curse because the curse is not totally a sexual thing. It starts with an appeal that makes the curse possible. There's a way about the way you move. The way you do things. There's an attraction, something that draws you in. It's a nectar, an unconscious aroma. Something you don't have to touch, but arouses the sinful nature of man. That's just like God to use whatever He wants for his ministry.

I just see it as a lesson. Yes, it was another man. It wasn't a lover, this time. Even though, there were times when the devil presented the thought, and the thought crossed my mind. It was just the devil trying to work the curse anyway he could. But, I know you don't mix business with pleasure. I knew how to handle my business. The curse couldn't keep me from taking care of my responsibility, with the exception of the boulder which was the making of a ministry. Plus, the shame of the curse made me feel I was unworthy of this man. You know, curses come complete with low self esteem.

This man lived in my house. He paid me rent. He helped meet my expenses by paying his rent. He was one of my kind, a military man. He was dependable. He paid his child support. He took care of his children, but he too was cursed. Oh yeah, he was cursed. Same curse, different person, different family, but the very same curse. Note, this same curse plagues many people because it derives from something God meant for good, and it is good, in the right context. All the handiwork of the devil. Is that why God sent him to my house? One who was going through the very same curse, and required deliverance. God knew I'd minister to every man I encounter closely, and he was chosen. He lived in my house. He actually came in my house, and attempted to seduce my child, my daughter, Ebony.

Prior to anything happening, God had me ministering to him. Every message I received from God, I shared with him, as I do now. I shared every word God gave me. But, this man lived in my house. Sometimes, I spent hours, whole mornings preaching. I didn't call them sermons, but I was preaching. It was God's word. Words that always lined up with whatever spoken Word, the Rhema, God had for the church that day.

Oh yes, Richard received a lot of Word. I shared much with him. Then, he witnessed first hand the turmoil of my being cursed. He was there through the boulder experience. He experienced it all. He saw me go through all of it with Christ. Oh yes, I went through every bit of it with Jesus. He was the forefront of my life, and Richard watched me cry out to God through it all.

Then, he was compelled to come onto my daughter, my 14 year old daughter. He lived in my house, and he was coming onto my daughter. Of course, a 14 year old may have felt this type of attention special. It had to be flattering to have an upstanding nice older guy attracted to you. There are so many things that come into play in the mind and flesh of a 14 year old, especially one who has a bloodline that was cursed with the curse of promiscuity.

Many things may have come to mind. Such as, if a man of Richard's stature is looking at me like that, it must be all good. A huge self-esteem builder, but Richard was cursed. The same curse I had, the curse of promiscuity. A curse of the flesh, and of course we know that nothing good is in this flesh. A curse that satan readily uses on many people. He used it on Richard. He looked at my daughter. At first, it was just to look. Don't you know, the devil put thoughts in his mind. I'm sure, Ebony had a remnant of my curse, and the nectar of my seed also had to be sweet. But, God, yes my Lord, brought all that to a head before it went that far, before it got physical. Then there was the test.

Of course, most people would think I should or would hate this man. The man that attempted to corrupt my seed. I can't hate him. I can't hate anyone. God has unconditional forgiveness for us, so I too, must have unconditional forgiveness if I'm who I profess to be, a child of God. God did say, let this mind be in you like Christ Jesus. In other words, practice what you preach. Understand me, I'm not making myself forgiven him. I just forgive him. I can forgive him because when everything went bad, he did exactly what he was called to do. What God wants all of us to do. He turned to our Father. He repented and asked God to forgive him. He already had it instilled in him. He had been ministered to for almost a year. Yes, he had, a solo ministry, for a year.

I had to do what God calls for His children to do. I had to show the true love of Christ. I couldn't seek revenge on my own. Vengeance is mine says the Lord. It belongs to God, and He makes everyone pay for all their wrongdoing. I didn't have to do anything. God will do it, and I know that so very well. You'll suffer the consequences of your choices, but the choice is all yours. God gave the choice to you. He has called heaven and earth to witness your choices, you reap the benefits of your decisions. Right or wrong. Good or bad. Life or death. Important note to remember is your choice not only affects you, but also your seed, generations to come. It was choices that created generational curses. A choice to be disobedient to God's Word.

In turn, I had to minister the same thing to my daughter. I had to minister forgiveness. I had to help her see that, everything happens for a reason. All that is done is done, and God is in control. We really have very little control because our flesh is constantly warring against the spirit. We do many things we don't understand, and we don't even know why we do them especially when we're functioning under a curse.

When you are willing to make a change in your life. When you are willing to accept Christ as being the one and only true God over your life. When you are willing to walk in this way and follow His way, then oh my God. You can't help, but forgive a child of God. God revealed this to me - unconditional forgiveness. His Word says, He is just and faithful to forgive you of all your sins, if you repent. His word is true. It's written in blood, Jesus' blood. I couldn't have done anything else. God is constantly making me over. This was yet another ministry. He did say, all things work together for the good...that's the good and the bad.

The day we went to court for this situation, there were many factors. Here was an E-7 promotable, who was supposed to pin on his E-8. He already had his date to pin on his rank. Who was the pillar of the military community. Who loved the Army, in fact, the Army was his life, somewhat of a God to him. He could get just about any female he wanted, but he liked them young. He was whorish, but he never brought that into my house. He was very respectable in my house, at least I thought.

Then, he does this stupid thing. This thing that inadvertently has cost him everything he held dear. You know, you can't put anything before God. Anything you put before God is considered an idol, a god. He did say, thou shalt have no other gods before Him. Sometimes we make our jobs, a god. Our homes, a god. Our cars, a god. Money, a god. We even make other people, a god. We make alcohol, drugs and so many other things, gods in our lives. You see, to make something a god means you put this thing before anything. You must have this thing. This thing is what you use to fill the void you have inside, or you think will fill the void. It can only fill it temporarily, but never to the extend God wants to fill you. Only God can, and only God will quench that insatiable thirst you have deep inside you. It's a void that can only be filled with the Holy Spirit of God.

Then, God gives you liberty after He fills the void. He knows as long as He comes first, and He is God in your life, you have liberty. You have freedom. You have anything you want, as long as it's in God's will and used for the glory of Him. His will is in His word. If His word says it, you can believe it because God stands by Himself, His Word. Everything contradictory to that is the lie satan has used to keep us trapped and in bondage. satan doesn't want us to see that God is God. He doesn't want us to see that God will truly love us for who we are, however we are, and despite whatever we've done. God loved us before the world was created. Before we fell in sin. Before sin was sin. He loves us at our best, and that's who and how we are at any given moment. He has an unconditional forgiveness.

There are no conditions on His forgiveness. All you have to do is recognize what you did, accept responsibility for your actions, and repent. Yes, repent, do a total 180 degree change from that wrong thing to Jesus. Come to Him. Admit what you did. The thing, I notice about people, is until you see you have a problem, recognize it, you can't do anything about it. Repentance is just a sign of recognition. You recognize you were wrong in some ways, shape, form or fashion. You recognize it, and are willing to ask for forgiveness, and allow God to change you.

It's your choice. God has given you a choice. Then, He called for all of us to be of like mind, to do the same things. To do as He did, to forgive our trespasses as we forgive those who trespass against us. He does. We must realize it's not the person committing the offense. We don't wrestle against flesh and blood, but against powers and principalities. Anything not of God, done in the flesh is governed by another force, another god, satan. We must love the person, and hate the sin, and the creator of the sin.

So, who are we? Are we God? Not to forgive. Yes, I forgive Richard for trying to seduce my daughter. I forgive him for allowing his curse to take control of him, and cause him to attempt to abuse my child. God gave me that child, and I know God protects His children. So, I was able to minister to my daughter to allow her to see we must have unconditional forgiveness for one another.

Yes, God had me minister to my daughter about the fact that she too had a choice. My daughter had already accepted Christ as her Lord and Savior. She is a child of God. It was her choice whether or not she would forgive Richard. God is the God of forgiveness. I ministered that to her, as she received the ministry of forgiveness first hand. Ultimately, it was her choice. She chose to forgive. She chose to forgive him of all his wrong doings. She chose to let go, and let God set him free from all bondage.

The day we went to court, Richard's estranged wife was there, as was his mother and her fiancée. On the other side, it was Ebony and I. Richard said his mother wanted to meet the woman who had been ministering to her son, and was able to forgive him. That let's you know, mothers know what their children are capable of. I walked over to where Richard was. We were late as usual. I introduced myself to his mother, and soon to be stepfather. I figured the female was his wife. There was no formal introduction made, so I didn't even think about it. I really wasn't happy with some of the things she had done. She had her 15 year old daughter steal from her father to gain evidence he was messing around, so she could file for a divorce under the grounds of adultery and possibly savor her portion of his retirement pay. Always remember, God doesn't like ugly. Two wrongs don't make a right, and we should never use our children.

We're talking about a Jehovah Witness, but what can I say? Let me stop - Lord forgive me and forgive them for they know not what they do. They can't see Jehovah had no witnesses, only messengers and the Law. I really don't understand how they say they believe in God, but can't believe He loved us enough to give His son for us to have life. Lord open their eyes, open their heart, open their spirit to see your son and know they can't get to you except they come through and by your son, Jesus. Lord bless them all.

The prosecuting attorney came up and greeted us, Ebony and I. He said he needed to talk to us. He tried to tell us that Ebony had to testify against Richard, but we were only there because we had to be there because we were summoned. It was not our intention to testify to anything. After all, we didn't call the police, Richard did. Children of God take all matters to God, not before this law, especially the law today which only knows one-sided justice.

So, he continued to tell us how she had to say this and that. She had to do it. I asked what if she doesn't want to do it? He gave us the reasoning that people who do what Richard was accused of doing, continue to do it, and he might do it to someone else. He said Richard needed to get help, and many other things. He went on and on with the help of the investigating officer.

All of a sudden, God stepped in. He got my attention. We were in a room full of people. They were all looking at us, Ebony and I. God silenced me and said, "This is your daughter. This is your ministry. You hold jurisdiction here. I gave it to you. No one can tell you what your daughter has to do. You need to fight for your daughter."

So, I told the prosecuting attorney, as a mother, my daughter doesn't want to testify. She has forgiven him, and I won't make her testify. We are children of God, and she says she doesn't want to testify. She has nothing to say. Then, he went on with his spill to us about she has too... Then, Ebony spoke up, and said she didn't have anything to say. She said she believed God changed him, and if it happened to someone else then they'll have to press charges. If he did it before, then evidently their case wasn't strong enough to convict him. She'd forgiven him, and she had nothing to say. At that point, Ebony felt really pressured. Yes, she was withstanding the burden of the worldly judicial system.

After talking to the prosecuting attorney, we went pass Richard and his family, out to the corridor where we prayed. I anointed Ebony and myself. We held hands and prayed to God. We asked God to show us what He wanted us to do. We asked Him to reveal His will in this situation, and to let His will be done. We asked Him to take control, and we left it in His hands. We believed God when He said where two come together, touching and agreeing on anything, it shall be done.

Then, Ebony said she had to speak to Richard. So, she went to him. He was standing by his mother, her fiancée and his wife. Ebony said, let me ask you a question. She asked, "Are you really sorry for what you did?" He said, "Yes." She asked, "You won't do it again, will you?" He said, "As God is my witness, I would never do it again." She said, she forgave him, and she wouldn't testify against him. She said she had nothing to say.

After we left their presence, we went to sit down where I laid hands on Ebony's head as she laid her head in my lap because she had a headache. I comforted my child, a mother's ministry.

At that point, Richard took off. He appeared to be in a state of urgency. Evidently, he went to strike a deal. Ebony didn't want to testify or even get on the stand. Until we were called in the courtroom, we didn't know what was going to take place. We just trusted God would give us the desires of our hearts.

They called the case. We all went into the courtroom and sat down. We all waited for our petitions to come to pass. Ebony's hope was that she did not have to take the stand and testify. I hoped the same for her, and that this would all be over. Richard hoped he wouldn't have to go back to jail.

When the judge came in, we all stood up. The prosecuting attorney started reading off a plea. Richard had pleaded not guilty to the sexual assault charge, but to a lesser charge of disorderly conduct. He took a 12 month sentence, suspended for time served which was two days, and he agreed to attend an attempted sexual offenders course, which was once a week for six months. Ebony didn't have to take the stand, and it was all over, for us, that is.

God had definitely intervened. We all got what we hoped for. I made sure I let the prosecuting attorney know God was in control when we left the courtroom. He too, got what he wanted which was for Richard to attend a sexual offenders course. Richard, indeed, did not go to jail, but don't you know, you will still pay for your wrongdoing. God promised you would, and He is not a man that He should lie.

Right now, he's going through the struggle of loosing his military career. satan can't do anything to him because he is a child of God, but God has to ensure he learns a lesson from his mistakes. So, sometimes the things you love most will be taken away. You may have to feel the heat before God will give you a release. You aren't getting off easy. God knows it's human nature, if you continue to get away with wrong doings, you'll never stop. You'll continue to try and get away with what you're doing. That which is keeping you from your purpose, His plan for you, to bring you to an expected end.

On the other hand, if you feel some heat and you learn a lesson, sooner or later, you'll quit and you'll get the full meaning. So none the less, I still minister to Richard. I give him whatever word God has called for me to give him. I think the Word for him, from me, is about over. He has to start his own journey. It's all a journey. A journey in the school of life, God's classroom, and God has a journey for each of us to under take and a way we should go. He has truly put me on a journey because now that I realize it, I have preached many sermons, to a solo audience, only to go to church and have that same message preached to me. God definitely is on one accord. Thank you Lord. He said, yes you had already ministered it, only you did it just for Richard. God knew he was going to need it because He said He would put no more on you than you could bear. God always prepares you for what you'll go through. You just don't know what it's going to be until you go through, but know that to go through means you're coming out on the other side, God's side. Hallelujah!

I thank you Lord. That was a side bar from my Father. They happen often. Anyway, know that when you're going through, God is setting you up. He is preparing you for your purpose in this life. Your ultimate journey, even though, that journey may take different directions from the one you have chosen. God has changed Richard's journey. The truth is the real man in this story has a name, and there is something in a name. This man's name tells me there's a calling on his life, and all this is just ministry for his calling. God does work in mysterious ways. He's just awesome.

CHAPTER TEN

THE TEST

I waited patiently for the Lord; and He inclined unto me, and heard my cry. He brought me up also out of an horrible pit, out of the miry clay, and set my feet upon a rock, and established my going. And hath put a new song in my mouth, even praise unto our God; many shall see it, and fear, and shall trust in the Lord. Blessed is that man that maketh the Lord his trust, and respecteth not the proud, nor such as turn aside to lies.
Psalm 40: 1-4 (KJV)

You know you can't have a testimony without a test, and not until you pass that test. God knows I truly have a testimony. Yes, the test came. Good one, too. You know, God must ensure you are His. He must ensure you deserve, and can handle all He has for you, which is the best this world can offer and eternal life in His Kingdom.

Yes, the test came. It was David. A twenty year old college student, home from school for the summer. He was seriously trying to holla at me. That's what the younger people say today when someone is trying to get with you on an intimate companionship level. I was tempted. I really was, but then I thought about Thomas, and I couldn't. It wasn't because of what I was going through with Thomas, but the pain he was going through. The pain Thomas was enduring made me hurt. I couldn't see anyone else getting all messed up by the curse. Finally, I had the awareness, the knowledge, and the power in and through Christ Jesus, to stop the drama.

I knew there was a curse on my life. I also knew I broke that curse in the name of Jesus. The devil had one last try to get me, but I cried out to my Lord, my Father, and He stood by His Word. He delivered me.

I had to inquire into the one the devil, or God, now that I look at it, allowed to use, to tempt me. I had to know why this young man was trying to get with me, or why he thought he was. What was his attraction? Just how does God work? How was He working this time? You have to know, I pushed it close, but when reality truly struck, I didn't move. I was curious because the desire was not gone. I just realized, I was cursed. The devil had been dictating my life through the curse, but it was over. Now, My Father had give me control. My Lord stated there would be no greater temptation as known to man, but He would give me a way to escape. He gave me a revelation into His mysteries. I realized the way to escape was just to have a made up mind. A mind that said, I want to be free from the wiles of the devil because all he wants to do is kill me. A spirit that knows I have the power of God living in me, and the devil had no power over me. I was not ready to die. I wanted to live in this life. I wanted to fulfill my purpose for God. I wanted to enjoy my Father, and allow Him to enjoy His daughter.

I had to try real hard to keep Christ in the fore front of my mind. Having a person half your age, at my age is truly a compliment. He was young, handsome, built, and on the right track. They seemed to get younger and younger. Just the thought of the capabilities of a younger man made me wonder.

That's residue from the curse. It attacks the mind. Boy, does it attack the mind. It fills it with all kinds of garbage.

I knew this young man's mother. She worked for me some years ago. I never knew she had a son. Even though, I wasn't in the habit of seducing people's children. She was a single parent, raising two children alone. She was a statistic, and the curse was trying to make her son one, too. Thank you Lord. I sure would hate it for one of my son's to get caught up in a curse, like the one that plagued my life.

I told him he didn't want to get with me because I was known to mess up a man's head. I told him, all the men that got with me, except one, ended up really messed up in one way or another. They were already broken, in different ways, and all I did was shatter them. I never mentioned the curse. I guess I really didn't want to scare him away. Ironically, I couldn't seem to minister to him. That was unusual. I never had a problem ministering and talking about my Father to anyone. I talked about the Lord to everyone, on any occasion. To tell the truth, we had no conversation of any sort. It was apparent to me, it was just a test.

He came by to see me, late one night. I had already gone to bed, but he was persistent about coming over. We just sat there watching television until he dozed off. Then, he went home. There was no pressure, no unrestrained desire. At that point, I knew I passed the test. I celebrated with a shout, a praise to my God. That's when God made me into a Mary. It wasn't until then that I could talk to David about who I truly am, a child of God. One on my way to my mission, fulfilling my purpose in this life for God.

That's when I found out he was raised right. His single parent mother raised a son who really wasn't looking for a mess, and knew how not to get into one. He knew what he wanted, and was willing to go after it. If that didn't work, he knew how to move on. He was very settled in mind and spirit. He even went to Bible study. That was my cue, I could minister to him and truly explain to him why he should be glad he didn't get tangled up with me. I thanked him for being who he was, and being able to pass the test. I told him I knew he had to be special. I've never had a man just walk away. No fuss, no fight, no struggle, no revenge. I wasn't offended or hurt. I was just relieved. There's an awesome peace that comes from acceptance. satan had lost all grips on my life. I passed the test. Thank you Lord.

    I pray many blessing for David because God used him in a mighty way. He puts me to mind of Samson who was beguiled by satan's deviousness through Delilah. Although, he gave into his desire, God wouldn't allow him to be defeated. He had to fulfill his calling, his purpose. As will David, I'm sure. God bless you David. Thank you Lord, my Father through many toils and strife, I have learned your will and I finally passed the test.

CHAPTER ELEVEN

CHOSEN TOO

And the Lord God said, It is not good that man should be alone; I will make him an help meet for him. And the Lord God caused a deep sleep to fall upon Adam, and he slept: and he took one of his ribs, closed up the flesh instead thereof; And the rib, which God had taken from man, made he a woman, and brought her unto the man. And Adam said, This is bone of my bone and flesh of my flesh: she shall be called Woman, because she was taken out of man. Therefore shall a man leave his father and mother, and shall cleave unto his wife: and they shall be one flesh. And they were both naked and not ashamed.
Genesis 1: 18, 21-25 (KJV)

Wouldn't you know my husband would deserve two chapters. After all, he is second in my chain of command. So, why shouldn't he have two chapters. That was then. This is now. God presented me to my husband and he recognized me. He made a choice, and then I made a choice. I made a choice a long time ago. My spirit recognized my husband from the very beginning. Like Tom Hanks recognized his lady in the movie, "You Got Mail," your other half, your set apart, will know you despite what the circumstances are. You just have to be open and aware enough to recognize and receive what God tells you in your spirit, not in your flesh. Then you just have to be patient and wait for God to do what He has allowed you to know He will do. What a God.

Myles Monroe says, God presents individuals for us to choose from, but we ultimately make the choice. My spirit chose John. He was chosen too.

I believe God has a counter part for you. He waits to see if your spirit will recognize that person when He presents them to you. If we recognize the one He has separated us from in the beginning His will has been done. He intended for us to have marriages made by Him to create seed made after Him, blessed seed, as we are. Adam, recreated, the way He intended it from the beginning.

I know it was God's will we met. God presented Eve to Adam. I came back from Desert Storm, the war, communing with God, in a land where you can be killed at the mention of the name of Jesus. We were having Pentecost, just experiencing all God's love. I had no intention of staying in the Army. In fact, I was trying to get out early. That's another battle I war, weight, but even in that, God has given me victory.

Anyway, I came down on orders to go to Germany. Overweight and tired, I was convinced by Monroe to stay in the Army, and go to Germany. We were on one of our "Get back together again" phases. I prayed about it. Yes, I sought God first. I prayed to God, if it was His will He would do whatever it took for me to go. You know He did. He motivated me to loose 30 pounds in thirty days. I reenlisted in the Army, and went to Germany.

I should have known by the events that occurred I would be in Germany by myself. I was alone, but God ensured I had my children. My girls went with me this time. He was preparing them for their ministries. All the passports, except Monroe's went through. So, when they should've come to Germany, they couldn't because he couldn't. I went to Germany. I found a place for us to live in one week. No thanks to Monroe. He was draining my bank account before I could make a withdrawal. Mind you, we didn't have a joint account. He had stolen checks from me before I left. Checks, he denied taking or even seeing. He was forging my signature, and taking the money I earned. I was in a foreign country, alone, broke, and cursed. That dreaded curse of promiscuity.

I was in the country for a week before the curse revealed itself. I knew I looked good. I had lost 30 pounds. I was on my own. I knew Monroe had done worse, and what he has never known wouldn't hurt him. I met a youngun - that's southern for very young one. I really mean young. I was 32 years old and he was 18. Somebody's child. No older men would approach me. Some guy told me it was because I revealed the fire in me which meant I was to hard to handle and too hot to hold. He said, older men were intimidated by me. I don't know if that's true, but they sure weren't biting.

I can say now the curse created something that was good. I say, I'm a freak. In all actuality, it just breathes God's word. It says the marriage bed undefiled, check out the Song of Solomon. I chose my husband, and he chose me too. No matter how introverted he seems. Our spirits recognized each other on our first meeting. Yet, I was being sexed by an 18 year old, even though, we had no conversation. Just to clarify, when I say sexed, it was only two times. A little bit of sin, a whole lot of sin, same, same.

It was Thursday after Valentine's day. We, my 18 year old and I, were supposed to meet at the Image, a German night club that catered to Americans. He was stationed in Baumholder, which is about 40 miles away from where I was. Without transportation, you had to depend on others, but everyone came down Thursday night. Straight to the Image. It was the place to be. Thursday night was ladies night with exotic dancers until 10 p.m. Two hours of men dancing for the ladies. All the ladies got in free. The night spent being with Americans, having a serious party. That's where I met my 18 year old lover.

My 18 year old lover didn't show up that night. It didn't matter, I love to party, and that's just what I did. I continued looking for him, but I kept flirting in the process and having a nice time alone. He was only a product of the curse. There was no love loss. Unlike the freudian female, I didn't have to feel you, to lay with you. My sexuality was that of a man, I just needed a fix. The curse of promiscuity was used to fill the void. The desire I had was a deep burning desire. It was like a drug, and I was the addict. I just needed a fix.

I met John in February after the show, I was feeling nice and hungry, and he stepped up to the bar and grill, and politely asked if I was in line. I said, no, and we started talking. It was small talk because John is a small talk type of guy. There was no line, no come on, just a real question for a real situation. Typical male, guarding his feelings, his heart, himself. Then, they played some Raggae music. I don't know, if I told you, but I have this fetish for island men. Monroe was from Panama. That isn't even an island. Maybe that's why, it was all messed up. The spirit of God had already let me know the man for me would come from the islands, and John is from the Virgin Islands. The devil presented Monroe as a sorry imitation. He's always trying to imitate what God has, is and does. The Word tells me he'll continue to imitate until the end of time as we know it.

We danced to the Raggae beat. I pride myself in my dancing ability or lack of, always being able to flow in the spirit, dancing to anything. A free spirit. I danced to that Raggae beat, like a real island child. Then, we spent the rest of the evening together. This island man captivated me. He fit the bill of the man I dreamed would be in my life. He was tall, dark, slim, and an island child. What more could I possibly ask for.

There is a dilemma for everyone going to Germany or anywhere overseas. You have to wait for your vehicle to get there, and mine was on it's way. It was in route. John offered to take me home, after he went all the way to Baumholder, 40 minutes one way. He had to take his friend back. He, too was stationed in Baumholder. The infantry was there, many men.

I enjoyed the ride. I had only been in Germany about three weeks, and I hadn't been anywhere. I was too busy setting up house for my family. Bright lights and Raggae music, which is really deep, if you listen to JAH. After all, that's God, at least that's what Psalm 68:4 says. Bet you didn't know that. So, check out Bob Marley, who was a prophet sent with a message for this time.

You know this is a side bar and it's being done in the edit stage, but God says go here and I'm obedient to God. I must tell you that it's in obedience that God blesses us, and if God wants you to have a Word from Him, if I were you I'd be sure and receive it. This is being written in the spirit, as is this entire book. But God's word for this moment is WATCH. Open your eyes to the things around you because He is using things only His children will be able to see to reveal Himself, and to tell us what time it is. Daniel says, He changes the times and the seasons, and there are about to be some changes. This is a spiritual thing that our intellect won't be able to get a hold on. There are messages in the movies, in the songs, in the drama, in the news, everywhere. You have to be open and let God speak to you. God said he would take the foolishness to confound the wise, and that's what He's doing today. So watch and pray. Jeremiah said listen, and hear what thus says the Lord. He speaks to His children, WATCH. This is the dawn of a new day.

God is birthing a revolution, a radical body of believers. It's party time. Time to get drunk on a new wine, the wine of the anointing. Anointed with the anointing that destroys every burden and breaks every yoke. We are in the day and age, where God said greater things we would do. Oh praise God, bless you Father, Hallelujah!! You know I could shout right now. I feel the fire, and it's all over me. Oh just take a minute and praise Him, shout Hallelujah!

Let's get back to my testimony because through it I have overcome. Hallelujah, I am naked and not ashamed. Nobody knows how much it cost to be me. But, John came home with me that first night. We made love the first night. I would say, we had sex, but it was more than that. We made love. Our spirits met. Like the Bible implies, we knew each other. I wanted him there, and I wanted to be there. It was more than just sex. I could feel his heart beat, even though, we were from two different worlds. He wasn't Americanized, and if I didn't know better, he may have been cursed too. The same one I have. He told me all his stories, and I read his windshield that said something that may constitute a person who's cursed. I really began to know him.

From that day, John and I were together. He gave me his car until mine got there. He knew I was married, but he continued to fill the void. Then, one month and a half in country, my mother-in-law had a massive stroke. I had to go back to the United States, and I did. I loved my mother-in-law like she was my own mother. She's really why I endeavored to say "I do" to Monroe. I wanted and needed a mother's love. I missed my mother just that much.

I supported Monroe while he was at his mom's house, financially and emotionally. Then, we had to go home to our children. Monroe just packed his bags and left, without considering anything, when his mom had her stroke. He totally forgot about the woman he left behind who was living with him in our house.

As we approached home, the vibes changed. I knew something was up. Something was wrong. It all came out. Monroe had another woman, and another drug habit. I was sending him money and he hadn't paid any bills. She moved her clothes into my house, into my closet, and my dressers drawers. He never thought I would be coming back there. Can we say, God had a plan. He denied everything, even though, one of our friends, who was also living in the house, told me the whole truth. Someone was finally tired of seeing me be used and abused. The whole truth about Ms. Janice, the other woman, was out.

My aunt died while I was home. My mother's only sister who surpassed the curse of cancer to see her children grown. The last one of my mother's siblings. Of course, Monroe couldn't show me any support. He had his own issues. Three emergencies in one, my mother-in-law's stroke, my aunt's death, and what I thought to be the final break up of our marriage. Even the Army thought that was a bit much. They wondered how could one person with stand such trauma. It was God. It came in three like the Trinity. There was no one else to turn to but to God. He did say, He would put no more on me than I could bear.

I paid my respects, and packed me and my children up to go back to Germany. Transportation moved us in one week. Now, that's God because the military transportation system usually takes at least a month to get someone moved, and I was out in a week. Monroe couldn't come if he wanted to. He had no passport.

John met the girls. He was like a father to them. A father they never had. Little did I know, he was making up for not being there for his own children. He cared for them like I would. He would even baby-sit my children while I was in school. They enjoyed him, and he enjoyed them too.

We spent time together, as a couple and as a family. It was

never pressed. I enjoyed him. He enjoyed me too. We lived free and trusting lives. When we were together, I loved him and loved on him like I have never loved any man because I never really loved any other man. He was very kind, in his own cynical way. We've never had an argument. We debate and he has his rules that were fair. Rule #1, John's always right, and Rule #2 says refer back to Rule #1.

Yes, our spirits met, but John was never willing to commit. That statement really seems funny now because John was always committed. I read a commentary by Romuald Wills, titled "How to Find a Good Man." Wills says, a man is committed if he is committed to a job, and outside community activities. So, he really is committed. It just wasn't God's time for us. He has a work to do in both of us. He is making John into the man he has to become to be with me, and making me into the woman He wants me to be for him because God wants a marriage made by Him that He can use for the glory of Him. God is delivering me from all my baggage and all the curses, I had acquired. He is making me into a virtuous woman for my husband, my Adam.

We have spent all our time apart, but the love we have for each other has never changed, even though, the curse was alive and very active. I love my husband. It's a love for the rest of my life. I thank God He allowed my spirit to recognize my husband, and my husband's spirit to recognize me. He's been hurt, but he confessed it with his mouth, and I was cursed. He has an unconditional love and forgiveness for me. Now you know that can only come from God.

I trust John. I don't put my trust in him. I truly and simply trust him. He knows me, and I know him. Only, I have yet to get him naked. Naked and not ashamed, like I have made myself in this book. In a marriage, a man and a wife need to be naked and not ashamed.

Bishop T.D. Jakes' has an awesome ministry for women in relationships. I highly promote and recommend it. He says, "The art of communication is the key. We both have different needs, so understanding is a ministry." He says, "We have to start talking to find out how fit a marriage is to be." I'm ready to start talking, can't you tell?

John was chosen, as was I, because we are one. The Word says, What God joined together let no man put asunder. God had set him apart just for me. God presented me to him, and his spirit recognized me even in a worldly state. We must remember, God can do all things. He is in control. God set him apart just for me, and made me into his wife. Bishop T.D. Jakes also says, "Who can find a virtuous woman?" He says, "She found herself." Then, God gave her a lover, her husband. The Lady, Her Lover, and Her Lord. Marriage, a relationship made by God, the way He wants it.

It's truly beautiful. God's love, and the love He wants us to have for one another, especially for your husband. I'm finally single. God has given me my husband, someone to love in the physical sense, which is the only way God can enjoy His creation.

Yes, marriage is us going back to the original state. The first state of man. Single, but not alone. An Adam. He said, He made them, male and female made He them. One mind, one body, one spirit. A three fold cord not easily broken.

God wanted us both to be in Him and whole, so He could use us. Don't you know, there's no power like the power in a marriage. Two touching and agreeing. I can't wait until God allows me and my husband to come together, and do His will.

Yes, I was chosen to be my husband's friend, his lover, his wife, and his help meet. Yes, John, you are chosen of God, and we have work to do. I love you.

CHAPTER TWELVE

HOW YOU LIKE ME NOW?

Then I looked and heard the voice of many angels, numbering thousands upon thousands, and ten thousands times ten thousand. They encircled the throne and the living creatures and the elders. In a loud voice they sang; "Worthy of the Lamb, who was slain, to receive power and wealth and wisdom and strength and honor and glory and praise!" Then I heard every creature in heaven and on earth and under the earth and on the sea, and all that is in them, singing; "To him who sits on the throne and to the Lamb be praise and honor and glory and power, forever and ever!" The four living creatures said, "Amen," and the elders fell down and worshipped.
Revelation 5: 11-14 (NIV)

Sometimes I really can't believe the awesomeness of God. I can't believe how He lives in me. It's unreal, and so so good. It's so good I just want to share it with everyone because everyone should be able to enjoy the love of God. Yes, love Him because He definitely will love you back. He really does love His children, His creations. Creations unlimited, each an original and unique design,

I thank God for my deliverance. I thank Him for finding me special enough to love me. Special enough to deliver me from all my wrongs. I thank Him for loving on me, and providing for my every need. I thank God for birthing a ministry in me, His ministry. I thank Him for finding me worthy enough to help His hurting people. I thank Him for giving me the heart to want to follow Him, and do all I can to be who He intends for me to be. I thank Him for all the amenities because He definitely is a giving Father. He takes good care of His children. I thank Him for allowing me to live in His vision, a vision beyond my greatest imagination. He did say, He would give us exceedingly abundantly more than we ask or think. Can you imagine that? I thank Him for joy and peace, my strength and comfort. I thank Him for my life. God I thank you.

You know, this that I'm feeling, and I do mean feeling because I am definitely feeling Him alive in me. It's really hard to describe. It really is beyond the imagination. I feel full. So full, like I'm about to burst, from the top of my head, to the tips of my toes. God has definitely filled that void in me, and it feels so good.

God has filled my cup to overflowing. I can't help, but minister to everyone I come in contact with, as God calls me to minister to them. I allow Him to use me however and whenever He chooses to. You know, ministering is just telling the truth, speaking the gospel, the good news. It's helping people realize Christ is the Good News, and all joy and happiness is in Him. He wants us to live in this life. He wants us to truly have heaven here on earth. You know, you really can, if you trust Him.

People, it's time to start trusting Him. Life as we know it, is going to change and time draws nigh. Like the scripture tells us, you don't want to be one of the maidens with no oil in your lamp. Christ is preparing a new generation, the Resurrection Generation. He is building this ministry to prepare for His return, so as many as will accept Him will catch that last flight. He is looking for you. He has given you the most crucial parts of His ministry, even through me, to bring deliverance in the lives of His children. It's all tricks of satan. It's time for God's people to open their spirits and recognize God wants so much more for them. He wants them to come home, to come to Him.

God has allowed me to see I can be real, with all my faults, because He loves me at my best. That's how I am at any given time, at any given moment. He loves me just the way I am. After all, He made me this way. He is the Potter, and I am the clay. He is continuously making and molding me into who He wants me to be. This process is a constant evolution into the beautiful, holy, pure, and sanctified vessel He desires me to be. A vessel He can use. I like being used by God. It's definitely not like being used by men because He truly loves me, and shows it in every way possible and then some.

Sometimes, I feel like a little child waiting for my Father, knowing He will come to me and hold me. Knowing He will whisper sweet words of wisdom in my heart and in my ears. All I want to do is please Him. Obedience is the key, and walking in faith is the window to His ministry. I have finally grabbed a hold of His faith. I know that pleases Him because He said without faith it is impossible to please Him. He also said by faith I could do all things. I can say to the mountain be moved, and it'll move. God knew we would create many mountains to climb and would need Him to be the footprints in the sand.

I have made my amends with all those I may have hurt, or who hurt me. It's so good to be free. It's good to be released from the bondage of unforgiveness. I have received His total forgiveness as He promised, an unconditional forgiveness. He has even shown me, we can forgive as soon as we make up our mind and heart, we just have to decide we want to. No, we may never forget what hurt us, but our hurt can be like a road. A road will always be there. You'll see it every day, but it doesn't mean anything to you. It doesn't affect your emotions, your spirit. It's just the route you have to take to get to where you're going, to get to the end of your journey. It's just a part of the trip. A trip down life's highway. A highway where you'll encounter good road, bad road, pot holes, and roads under construction, but you can't allow the condition of the road to keep you from your ultimate destination. You have to make the choice to take another route, if the condition of the road is deterring your journey.

God finally made me into a Mary, no more Martha. Mary knew who Jesus was from the beginning. She loved and worshipped Him, and He loved her back. She put her total trust in Him. She knew in Him was all power. Don't get me wrong, Martha loved Him too, only she didn't fully understand that He is God. She didn't understand, there was no impossibilities in Him. She was like many of us. She had a form of godliness, but denied the power thereof, that's Word. God wants all of us to be Mary's, Job's, David's, Rahab's, and the list goes on and on. He has no respect of persons. To Him we're all the same, and He wants us all to be the same. He wants us to stop playing church and be a church, His body, one mind, one body, one spirit, all on one accord, manifesting the overflow and power of the Holy Ghost with signs, wonders, and miracles.

You know, the church as we know it, the building fellowships, today's Christians have made a mockery of Christ. They have put more people in bondage. They've truly been busy, remember Being Under Satan's Yoke. They have deceived God's people. Many of them live with anger, guilt, shame, and feeling unworthy of God's love. They continue to live out the Law, however, just like in the biblical days, they can't live the whole

Law. The Word says, if one lives one part of the Law, they must live the whole Law. Only Christ could fulfill the Law. The Law is perfect, and only Christ is perfect. After all, He is God, born of a virgin, and wrapped in sinful flesh. He came here just to show us, with God we could live this life. We can perform all the deeds He performed, knowing one day we will meet Him face to face.

It's time for all God's people to come together. It's time to tear satan's kingdom down. It's time to come out of the buildings. The harvest is in the fields, and it's ready for picking. God needs laborers to reap His harvest. He is stirring up the gifts and making ministers of our children. Parents it's time to start ministering to your children. God said train a child. Yes, raise your children in the way they will go. If you're raising them in Christ, the Truth, they'll go the right way. All you have to do is plant the seeds, He'll water them and make them grow. You must commit your children to God. Our children are dying. It's up to us to provide them with life. They are the X-Generation, X-tra special. They are also the Y-Generation, the Yoke breaking generation, only to birth the Resurrection Generation.

God has allowed me to see most everything He wants me to be and do. It's inside of me. All I have to do is rely on Him to water the seeds He planted and wait for them to bloom, that they may produce more seed. He did say be fruitful and multiply. This is the way He multiplies His children, through the ministry of reconciliation. He has called all of us who have accepted Him into our lives to perform this ministry, reconciling people unto Him. It's not about me or you. It's about our brothers and sisters who are unloved, broken, sick, substance dependent, and religious. It's about all those who don't know Christ in the fullness of His glory. He did say, do unto others as you have them do unto you, esteem others higher than yourself, and to love your neighbor as yourself. That's really very simple to understand, but not very many seem to acknowledge, that to love Christ, I must love all my brothers and sisters. No matter what color skin they're wrapped in. God made us in His image. Ultimately, we are spirit beings just covered in a unique design, flesh, so we in this world may be able to recognize each other.

The sad thing about not recognizing the commandments Jesus gave us is we hinder our own blessings when we don't love our brothers and sisters enough to help them see the truth, the marvelous light. I can't reach the top without you getting there with me. With the love of God in me, that is my greatest desire, to see all His people come to the full knowledge of the truth, to allow God to love them, and bring their purpose, their ministry, to fruition, to an expected end.

Sometimes, I want to cry. When I think of how we must hurt our Father by not allowing Him to love, protect and provide for us the way He wants to. It has to really hurt Him when He sees us making the wrong choices and knowing we will be hurt and broken by our choices, but it's our choice. He has given us free will, just like a parent who watches their children grow up and seek their independence. We would hope they would talk to us and with us and listen to us as we share with them what we know is right. Share that which will ultimately be the best for them. I ache when I watch my children suffer for making the wrong decisions. I know I must let go and let them learn from their mistakes as I had to learn from mine. I thank God all things work together for the good of them that love Him and are called according to His purpose. I also thank God that everything satan means for bad He can and will take and make it for His good. He did say the battle was His and if we hold our peace and let Him fight it, we can be no less than victorious. Victory is mine says the Lord. satan is and always has been a defeated foe, yet people still continue to follow him. At this point, I really don't understand why, when God has so many good things for those who receive Him, and allow the master architect to build on a solid foundation. A foundation constructed by His Word, set up on Jesus, and sealed by the Holy Ghost, making them into someone truly marvelous.

I am a church on fire and God is allowing me to flow in His spirit with the fruits of the spirit. His precious gifts are working in and through me. He allows me to look at people and see their spirit. Evangelist Belinda Moss says it's reading your mail. It's not me, it's He that lives in me. I just allow it to be so. It's my choice. God has me laying hands on people in stores and parking lots, anywhere He calls for healing. Hurting people are everywhere. We must always be ready to do His will, hear His voice and immediately obey. God even had me lay hands on a dog and immediately He healed his broken leg. It was just a test for the people in the house, but even for that to remain, faith must remain intact. You know, God will always pass the test. He's not like us, He's perfect in and of Himself.

God has me working in my ministry, without the total set up because He presents the unborn to me. He allows me sometimes to see the babies in the womb, in the spirit. He tells me to bless them, and I do. I pray God's purpose be stored in their hearts and minds as they develop in the womb. I pray their spirits be nurtured and grow. It's time, the Resurrection Generation is on it's way, and they are touching ground as we speak.

He has given me the vision for what I should do with this ministry, where I should locate myself and everything. It's all about people helping people for God. Pushing people up to push them out into the fields, to reap the harvest. Sounds like discipling to me, but that's the task of being chosen. The Word says many are called but few are chosen. Those few must be about their Father's business, sowing seed and reaping the harvest, even in fields they did not sow. God is ready to bless His people. It's time to enter into the Promise Land, the land of milk and honey. God said His people would be the head and not the tail and the time draws nigh for the reapers to over take the sowers.

I just thank God He snatched my life and saved me. I thank Him for choosing me, and giving me the hurt that allows me to invite you into the kingdom, for out of Jesus pain, his blood, sweat and tears, we have the right. I invite you into God's true fellowship, His body, the church. God wants us to be real. You no longer have to make believe. God is ready and wants to show Himself. He wants to teach you what you think you already know. You have to come as a child. Humble yourself and sincerely invite Him into your life. He said if my people who are called by my name would humble themselves, seek His face, repent and turn from their wicked ways, kneel down and pray, then He would seek heaven and heal the land. For God's sake must someone nail you to a cross to make you realize He made you for Him, and He can and will do all He said He would. I keep telling you, He's not a man and He cannot lie.

God said in these last days, He would pour out His spirit upon all flesh. Your sons and daughters shall prophesy and the old men shall dream dreams and the young men shall see visions. It's happening right now, even today, as we speak, prophetic words are going forth. Prophecies are coming to fruition. God has allowed me to minister to a fifth generation Muslim, who is just a Christian waiting to happen. That was plain and clear just the other day, through the life I live, and the ministry I give. This Muslim walked into my house and said, Do you like my T-shirt? This is what it had on it:

SEVEN
By Jomaro F. Kindred

The battle of Good and Evil has been written in the scrolls of time
Echoes of the fallen scream within my mind and while the tears of mankind renders me blind
This battle has been fought since the beginning of time
I look within and find the spirit to shine
And I look in the sky and know who has mine
So I stand absolute 360 degrees complete
and I fear no evil because I know you're obsolete
don't fear the dark side because I recognize deceit and since day one I know we would meet
and I would stand victorious because I know no defeat

God is control, charity, zeal, content, joy, humble, love
satan is lust, pride, wrath, envy, sloth, greed, gluttony
(Illustrated in a circle around God defeating satan)

Look at God. Look at God. He has no respect of persons. He calls who He wills. Look out religions because it's time for God to do a new thing. People are going to receive the truth. The truth is God is God. There is none before Him, and none after Him. He is the creator of all things, and all things were created by Him for Him. And because He is God, He felt compassion on a sinful world, and wrapped Himself in sinful flesh. He walked this earth thirty three years, healing the sick, mending the broken hearted, restoring life, and setting an example for us to follow. Then, He allowed Himself to be persecuted, lied on and betrayed, and He never said a mumbling word against His persecutors. He was crucified for you and for me. He shed His blood on Calvary for the sins of the world, for those past, present and future. He even sent back His spirit, His Holy Spirit, to live inside us, to comfort us, to keep us, and guide us. So, we might be able to live in this life, and have life more abundantly.

It's your choice, you can be like me, and be FREE, naked and not ashamed, or you can stay in bondage, never able to fully grasp the love and the riches in glory God has for you. It's your choice. All I can say is, How you like me now?

If you decide you want to have what I have, and live in this life, fulfill the purpose God put you here for, and allow your seed to grow and multiply, then all you need to do is make a sincere decision that you want to give your life to Christ. Then be obedient to His Word. The Word says in Romans 10:9, If you confess with your mouth the Lord Jesus and believe in your heart God raised Him from the dead, you shall be saved. It goes on further to say, that with the heart man believes unto righteousness and with the mouth confession is made unto salvation. It's just that easy to be saved. I can't lie to you, and tell you your future will be a bed of roses. God has to make you, mold you, and clean you up. As you can see from this ministry, it consist of delivering you from satan's handiwork, and preparing you for your ministry. There will be trials and tribulations, but He said count it all joy. Your joy is your strength, and He will give you peace. Peace the Bible says surpasses all understanding. The peace you get will allow you to go through any trial and be okay. He said, If you abide in Him, and His words abide in you, you can ask whatever you will, and it shall be done. Who couldn't and wouldn't want to serve a God that loves you just as you are, but too much too leave you that way. A God who will supply all your needs according to His riches in glory.

God is awesome, and He reigns forever. Won't you give your life to Him today. Be blessed, as I pray God's blessing upon everyone who reads this ministry. I pray you accept Him, and go forth and do His will. Like Jesus said to the deceased maiden,

— Cynthia A. Williams —

Talitha Cumi, which means Damsel arise, come forth. There's a new day dawning. I pray all those not in the faith, and those that are bound by traditions, wake up and see the light of day. God loves you, and I do too. Be blessed.

CHAPTER THIRTEEN

SET YOUR HOUSE IN ORDER

And if any man hunger, let him eat at home, that ye not come together unto condemnation. And the rest will I set in order when I come.
1 Corinthians 11:34

I really thought the book was finished. I should have known God was not through. After all, He is constantly working to make us into who we were called to be, ministers of reconciliation. This book is written for the deliverance of God's people to help you recognize that God's hand is in everything, the good and the bad, but He loves us despite the fact, and will see us through it all, if we put our total trust in Him.

God has opened up a big can of worms by touching on small portions of my life. He uses what He allowed me to go through to show His people, no matter what, no matter how dirty and nasty things seem to be, there is always hope, if your hope is in Him.

He has shown me there's nothing to be ashamed of because He's our Father. He'll love us through our struggles, but we must be honest with Him and ourselves. We must be honest enough to recognize and admit we are human, and living in this world is a battle, but no battle is too big for God. Through this ministry, He is allowing the world to see, He can and will deliver you from all your infirmities, but you must seek Him first.

He just wants His children to come to Him. He wants them to ask Him for His help, and diligently seek Him in all things because He can provide an answer to every question, every situation. He is the answer to everything. He is God, and in Him all things come together.

God doesn't want His children to live in condemnation, poverty, abuse, or anything of the sort. These are tools of the devil. satan wants us to condemn ourselves and others. He knows as long as we live our lives in condemnation, we'll never see the truth. We'll never receive the promise. We'll never enter into the Promise Land God has set apart for us, right here on earth.

God knows what we hunger for. He knows we're in this world. He knows we seek the things of this world, even though, His Word says, set not your affection on the things of this world, but He knows we do, or He wouldn't have said it. You must understand God knows what you need, want and desire. He is going to supply all your needs, if you trust Him. He wants to give you the desires of your heart, which is much more than this world has to offer. We must stop depending on man, ourselves, money, or anything else, except Him because it all belongs to Him. He holds this world in the palm of His hand.

God wants to do so much for His children, but He is held at bay by the motives of our hearts. We can no longer be selfish and think only of ourselves. God blesses us to be a blessing to others. He blesses you to do His will. He says many times in His word love your neighbor as yourself. He wants us to esteem others higher than ourselves. When we pray to God as Jesus taught His disciples, it's not about me or you, it's about us because He is OUR Father.

God is setting His house in order. He is preparing a new kingdom of people. He has shown me, the time is short. He wants His people, those called by His name, the Christians, church folk, to stop justifying themselves, and making excuses why they are disobedient to His word, and get it right. God is preparing a Wedding and bidding His people to come. The Word tells us, His people were unworthy. So, the invitation was taken to the highways and by-ways: the routy teens, the drug addicts, the prostitutes, the homeless, the lost, anyone so broken that they have no other choice but to believe God and put their total trust in Him. Anyone willing to hear what God has to say, and then be obedient to His word. He that hath an ear, let him hear what the Lord says.

God wants those people who say they know Him to humble themselves, pray, seek His face and turn from their wicked ways. I know you heard it before, but it can't be said enough until you realize that God will stand by His word, seek Heaven, forgive our sins and heal the land. We should be on a mission. This is about His people setting things in order until He comes. What more could we ask for? The very God Himself is pleading to do our bidding, to give us the life He wants us to have, not wanting for anything, just basking in the glory of Him. People seeking to do His will and being blessed with His joy and peace. A joy and peace the world can't even understand. I don't understand who couldn't or wouldn't want to turn to a God like this. Then, He gives you His spirit to comfort and keep you, as you take on the wiles of the devil, in your daily journey.

There are steps, a process, we all must go through to receive the total blessing of God. But before you can even start the process, you must be willing to hear God, and be obedient to His word. God is not slack in His promises. He is preparing His church to reap the harvest.

You see, God doesn't need any of us to do anything for Him. God can always find someone to do what you choose not to do. Look at Moses, who couldn't go into the Promise Land because of His anger, and disobedience. God just chose Joshua to step up to the plate. God wants His creation to be saved, and come into the Promise Land. He wants His children to develop the kind of love He has for us, an agape love, unconditional. He wants us to live in the overflow of His holy spirit, constantly pouring out what He wants to put in us, His word, His ways, His will, His love.

God delivered me. I am in the overflow. When I open my mouth, the abundance of my heart speaks. It pours out it's contents. It's constant. It's not a front, and it's awesome. I can't deny who I am, or whose I am because the very God lives freely in and through me, through and by His holy spirit. I understand, pray without ceasing, seek Him in all things, and doing His will. It's not a good idea, it's a God idea. Everything in God is good, even, His thoughts about us, and His plans for us.

You should know after my deliverance, God is now preparing me for my ultimate purpose in Him. He is setting things in order. He is getting my house in order. The testimonies continue to grow, daily. What others call burdens, God has shown me are blessings. They are a chance to take the test and pass. A chance to reveal God's power to work for and through His children. A chance to allow others to see God's word and His will at work. God is constantly educating me in His ways. He is teaching me to see Him in everything.

The house, God gave me, He has filled with a female and her four children. They are homeless, but know that except by God's grace, we're all just a paycheck away from being homeless. She is my spiritual equal, although she has a totally different personality, character and demeanor, and God is still in the process of taking her to where He wants her to be in Him. She's quiet. Our spirit's are on one accord, seeking God's perfect will for our lives and all those we encounter. That's just like God to fulfill what He presented at the Woman Thou Art Loosed Conference 99. Bishop T.D. Jakes noted that satan has done everything in his power to keep the women of God from coming together because he knows they know and understand one another. satan knows if the two would ever come together and cry out to God, walls, his demonic delusions, would be torn down. There's a power pack in the house, two women, studying God's word, and seeking to do His will.

Then, God allowed both of us to see why our lives, at this point, are in a state of famine. He has shown us that sometimes it's not you, but who you allow to come into and remain in your life, to use you. He also wants to see just how we will go through the famine. He wants to see if the spirit of Job exist in His daughters. Then, there's Jonah, yes Jonah, who in his disobedience was causing the whole ship to sink. It wasn't until they inquired of God did they realize Jonah was the cause for the ship sinking. They had to get Jonah off the boat to survive. Then everything was all right because Jonah ultimately fulfilled his purpose.

There are times when our helping hearts and hands hinder the plans God has for some of His people. When the children of Israel stopped receiving the daily manna from on high, God told them to go out and make their own provisions. Sometimes, you just have to let go and let God take control of those you care enough about to carry. You will look like the bad guy, but you must get out of God's way. God made it clear, to get your house in order, you must get Jonah out the boat, and don't look back. Don't be like Lot's wife. Trust God, and know He will take care of all His children.

God has also shown us how He will ensure His seed gets what He intended, even if, He has to replace those who were originally supposed to do the job. We know that it is His seed because the anointed and the blessed can only bring forth anointed and blessed seed, despite how the devil makes it look. You see, this female has a spirit like my daughter's father, humble, kind, meek, caring, and loving. Only, he is so full of anger, he can't fulfill his purpose in his children's lives. The daddy of this female's children is a soldier, who is cursed, a curse I know all too well. So, her children will ultimately receive what God intended them to have because of me being a soldier, having the same hard and disciplined demeanor. A facsimile of Basic Training. Consequently, I was assigned to fulfill the role of her children's father, to minister discipline for an appointed time. God gave His children what He wanted them to have from the beginning, and a ministry too. There goes God and His mysterious ways again.

For me, it's a challenge. I felt a strong desire to make things right. I have a passion for the welfare of the children, all children. I really have a deep desire for the teens of today. A desire that causes me to ball up in knots with birth pains. Pains that cause me to cry and wail out to God for their protection, their salvation, their future in Him brought to fruition. After all, the teens of today are the elders of tomorrow, the elders for the Resurrection Generation. Their purpose will be to mentor and minister to those young preachers, prophets, teachers, parents, evangelists, etc.

Wouldn't you know, God has brought me a family, placed them in my home, children, who call for a serious ministry of discipline. One night, God said to me, "Don't' give up and don't give in. If you can't rule your own household, how can I entrust you with mine?" Then, I read it in His word, confirmation, that same night. God is awesome.

The biggest testimony is God's preparation for me. He has used me in all my job areas to minister to His people, to plant seeds. The job I am presently on, he is truly setting everyone up. God is preparing a camp for His unborn seed. He has cleaned house in this OB/GYN Clinic. He has set His people in places to minister to the mothers of the unborn. God even presented me with a mural. I drew it on my ministry room wall. The "Unborn Babies," large and mega size, beautiful babies, all races with innocence in all the faces: Faith, Love, Hope and Peace. God is preparing the Resurrection Generation. He allows me to minister to the staff freely. He is truly setting things in order. But now, my spirit tells me, I'm packing up and getting ready to go. God is going to set me apart to prepare and get my ministry started. It's time to go evangelize, and minister to God's people, to reap the harvest.

God has made provisions for my children. For the first time in my military career, I have everything situated for my children, without any struggle. God's people willing to watch over my children's spirits. People helping people for the purpose of God. Laborers together for God.

God sent an anointed covering, a wonderful man of God, a Pastor with a passion for God's people and a first lady that is also a minister, a marriage, where two can come together and touch and agree on whatever the will of God is. Now that's armed and dangerous. satan watch out.

God is working, setting my house in order, so I can do my part in setting His house in order until He comes, and He is coming soon. The Resurrection Generation means Jesus is coming back. That generation is in the wombs of many right now as we speak.

God says it's time out for playing church. It's time to be a church and fulfill your purpose. He'll allow you to come out of the wilderness and enter into the Promise Land. I pray God's blessing upon you. I love you. Know that if you are reading this book, God is preparing you for something He wants you to do. I pray God free your mind and body. I pray your spirit receive what God has for you. If I were you right now, I would ask God to knock me right out of myself, that I would truly absorb in my spirit what He has predestined for me, for my life. It is a supreme privilege to have the very God, Jehovah, Jesus, the Almighty, the Great I Am, the Alpha and Omega, the Beginning and the End, the Present, the Past and the Future, call you out. Personally choose you to fulfill your destiny, and be able to live in this life, with His power in you. Enabling you to do all things, and have all things that you may share your blessings with others, so they may know the God we serve. So, they may know He loves His children. He yearns for them just to see Him as He is, for who He is. He's God. God all by Himself. Receive the Word. Seek Him today.

CHAPTER FOURTEEN

GUARD YOUR HEART

Keep thy heart with all diligence; for out of it are the issues of life. Put away from thee a froward mouth, and perverse lips put far from thee. Let thine eyes look right on, and thine eyelids look straight before thee. Ponder thy path of thy feet, and let all the ways be established. Turn not to the right hand nor to the left: remove thy foot from evil.
Proverb 4:23-27 (KJV)

My brothers and sisters, God has used my life as an example for you to see that it's okay to confess your faults. It's okay to admit your wrong doings, to strip yourself naked before Him because He loves you. He has made us realize that even in our nastiness, like the prodigal son in the pigpen, He loves and longs for us to come to Him. In whatever condition we're in, even in our mess, He'll still embrace us in His loving arms.

Sometimes you have to get really messy to appreciate His love and unconditional forgiveness. Sometimes you have to be a mess to appreciate getting naked, getting clean. God is our Father. He is ready and willing to wash you, to mold you, to make you, but you must keep your eyes on Him. You can't worry about what people say. You can't allow people's talk and gossip to control you. Only God can save you, and give the life He promised you. Let them talk. God knows who you really are. He knows whose you are, and where you're going.

Christ was crucified for your sins. He shed His blood so you might be washed clean. He gave you the right to live, however, even His crucifixion was open and public. His suffering was an open book for all the world to see, as yours too may be. That's part of the inheritance of Christ, and you are His royal heir. Some nail prints you won't be able to hide, but that's all right because there is a balm in Gilead. God is healer, and His word says, He heals the brokenhearted.

You see, when you strip yourself naked, all the wounds, open sores, lacerations, abrasions, burns, infections of your past and even your present will be open and oozing. A broken heart leaks issues. You must allow the healing virtue of God, through prayer and supplication, wash the wounds, empty your heart of all those issues and allow them to be healed, to be sealed, so they leak no more.

After all is said and done, you must guard your heart. The enemy is devious, as you have witnessed through my testimonies, my washing. He will do whatever and use whoever to get to your heart. He doesn't want your house, your car, your children, your career, he wants your heart. He wants your peace. The peace only God can give. The peace that surpasses all understanding. That peace that allows you to sleep when your whole world is in utter chaos. He knows once he gets your peace, you'll lose your focus. Your focus will be on him, and not on Jesus, the giver of life. He knows your focus will be on the cares of this world, the unpaid bills, the empty refrigerator, the bad evaluation on the job, everything except Christ. Guard your heart. It is the ultimate focus of his attack.

In the last couple of months, I've received the same Word, over and over and over again. It plays continuously in my mind, and permeates my dreams. Bishop Jakes, Kenneth Copeland, Taffi Dollar, Joyce Meyer, Rod Parsley and the list goes on, but it was coming from everywhere, the very same Word. God made it so very clear. Saints, it's vital that you GUARD YOUR HEART.

I realize now after setting my house in order, it's my heart satan has been trying to attack. I have said it several times in this book. The only reason I believe God has seen me through all I've been through is because of the heart He put in me, and now I know it to be true. satan knows I have the love of God in my heart, and I allowed the brokenhearted to touch my heart. Wrong answer. That's not to say, I should turn my back on those in need, but I can't allow them to impart burdens to distract me from the perfect will of God for my life.

Evangelist Tim Story says beware of foolish entanglements, those demonic forces you allow in your inner circle. Those people you allow to touch your heart. Everyone couldn't go behind the veil, which goes to say, you can't allow just anyone to get into those areas in your life that affect your very being. Even in the Old Testament days, there were degrees to which everyone could go according to their standing in God. Lord have mercy, and He does.

God said, guard your heart, place armed guards around your heart. Like a crown jewel has a security system always watching, always observing everyone that approaches the jewel. No one can touch or steal the jewel as long as the guards are on duty. It's a twenty four hour duty. The guards must be diligent. The Word says, keep thy heart with all diligence. The same diligence Christ talks about when He says, He is a rewarder of those that diligently seek Him. Seeking Him too is a twenty four hour job.

God is good. He is awesome. He has given you His spirit to teach you, to lead you, to guide you, if you walk in Him. He has charged angels to be at your beckon call, if you charge them. He has given you Himself, through His word and prayer, if you study and pray diligently. He has given you a full security system. No charge, it's already paid in full. Jesus paid the price. We, His children, touched God's heart, and Jesus gave His life. That's the cost of allowing satan to touch your heart. You pay for it with your life.

This may be the most important chapter in the book because it takes effect after you have been healed. Your heart is clean, and you are being purged. Set free from all those infirmities that plague your life. You are being set free to do God's will. Your heart will live forever. Everything God put in you is in your heart. So, you must guard your heart with all God put in you. Set armed guards around your heart. In this passage, that's what the word "keep" means.

Be careful who you allow to speak to you, or what you hear. Be careful what you allow to get into your heart, your spirit. Be watchful of evil thoughts that come into your mind, or that others present to you. It's time to do spiritual warfare. Bind, rebuke, and cast them out quickly. Don't give satan a foothold. Don't even let him get his toe in the door. Watch the influences you allow in your house, around your children, in your presence. Judge the tree by the fruit it bears. Don't let your heart go out to just anyone with a pitiful story. satan is just waiting for you to drop your guard, so he can kill you. He has an assignment, and it's got your name on it.

Bottom line, it's time to sell out. Your life is at stake. Guard your heart. You must take back all the devil stole from you. You must gird your tongue. You must speak only that which God has given you to speak, for out of the abundance of the heart the mouth speaks. Fill your heart with God, and you will only speak love and truth. You must keep your eyes on Christ. Keep them focused on Him, straight ahead, and you won't be tempted by the things around you. You must only step out on those things that are certain. In other words, seek God first, and follow His will for your life. You must establish a relationship where you hear and know your Shepherd's voice. Then, you must stay on the path. Don't turn to the left or the right. His word says, He leads you in the paths of righteousness for His name sake. Most of all, remove yourself from evil. Don't entertain evil, don't listen to it, don't speak it, don't do it.

God is building a church, His body. It begins with the heart. God said, Who shall ascend into the hill of the Lord? He that has clean hands and a pure heart. Repent, Confess Your Sins, Be Washed in His Blood, Receive the Gift of the Holy Ghost, Be Delivered and Set Free, Guard Your Heart, and Live.

CHAPTER FIFTEEN

THE ULTIMATE CHOICE

According as He hath chosen us in Him before the foundation of the world, that we should be holy and without blame before Him in love.
Ephesians 1:4

Yes, I'm one of those women, but if you haven't ventured into the book of life, the Bible, I need to tell you that all those women were saved, redeemed and ultimately washed in the blood. You read the story, you lived with me through the curses, the heartaches and the pain, what satan meant for evil, God, our Father has made good. You see, I realize God has been working out His purpose in me. Now I am delivered and set free. What seemed like my choice or my choosing were never my choice, but His choice.

It was His choice that I go through the pain and turmoil of a life that should be greeting me with six feet of earth on my face, but we serve a God who chose to redeem us, yes, you and me, before the foundation of the world. My God, if our earthly parents could or would have come close to what our heavenly Father has done. Through it all, He protected me, He led me, and He guided me. He knew there was nothing and no one who could keep me from what He had preordained for me.

Be assured I'm not special. I'm just like you, only now I am a child of God, a child of the King. An adopted daughter. Wouldn't you know that the adopted children are hand picked, they are wanted by the one who desires deeply to love them unconditionally. I'm no longer a babe striving to have my needs met, not caring about anyone else but myself. My crying days are over because just like a babe, I learned that even though I would fall my Father's hand was right there to pick me up because His desire and good pleasure is for me. All I have to do is trust in Him with all my heart and lean not to my own understanding. It didn't and doesn't matter what I do or what I've done because my Father doesn't see any of that, all He sees is the blood of His son, Jesus. His only begotten son, that He loved so much He allowed Him to die for you and me.

This life as a child of the King is awesome. It's unreal how our Father uses everything to make Himself known to us. I asked you how do you like me now? I should have been asking satan that question; after all, he is the only one, along with those that choose to follow him, that will feel the true wrath of God.

Now I see why he tried so hard to destroy me and my brothers and sisters in Christ. He never wanted us to realize that living, and I mean living, like our Father proposed in John 10:10, is easy. It's as easy as waking up every morning because you accomplish that by the measure of faith and grace our Father has given each of us, and He gives each of us new mercies every day.

People talk about the will of God, but little do they know that every day you live, walk and breath despite what you do, unless you are in total disobedience to the Father, you are in God's will. We are living out the book of life, and He is bringing us to our expected end only now we are in the end times. That's why so many movies, books and preached messages are revealing the prophecies, all those things spoken by man that have to come to pass before Christ's return.

I could say I made the choice, but I can do nothing of myself and I take no credit because ultimately it was His choice. He knew before I entered my mother's womb that I am a Prophetess, chosen to speak for Him. He knew the seeds He planted in me. I am chosen to seek not my own but yours, your salvation. Chosen to be about my Father's business. Blessed to be a blessing.

I am that vessel made of clay being filled each and every day. He is filling me until I overflow because He said He would pour out His spirit on all men, and His sons and daughters would prophesy. Yes, in this day, speak for Him, be His mouthpiece in this world. I am a living witness that we are prophets of our own lives. Our words, His words are life, if they are uttered from His spirit within you. Just that statement alone if actualized will bring about a revolution in your life and those around you. You can't tell me you're not tired of living in a world captivated by satan filled with crime, abuse, murder, debt, homelessness, poverty, adultery, lying, depression, sickness and disease and the list goes on and on. You see, God spoke and the world came into existence. Jesus said He gave us His words, the very word of God. Can't you see? Can't you hear your Savior calling?

When you get right down to it, it's all about love. Love conquers all. That's a cliché', but it's true. It was God's love for us that He gave His only begotten son, that means that is the only one, there will never be another. You have to really love someone to give them something you deeply love, something that can never be replaced. Then Jesus, a man in the flesh like us, just like you and me, loved us so much He gave His life for us. Only He wasn't quite like us because He was innocent, totally without sin, He knew no sin. Despite His innocence, He was beaten beyond recognition, blood poured from His pores, He was spit on and ridiculed, thorns poked in His head, and nailed to a Cross. He was hung up naked for the world to see, and He never uttered a mumbling word, knowing that all He had to do was say, " Father save me," and it was done. Now that's love. But His love was even deeper than that. He gave up His spirit, so we would have power to live, power to love, yes love one another. This love isn't an emotion, it isn't a feeling, it's an unconditional state of being resulting in unselfish action.

The church, those in those building fellowships, denominations they call themselves, more like demon nations, has severed the word of God. They pick and prod at the Word. Not all, but most, have yet to realize the simplicity of the gift we were given. Instead they still persist in living under the Law, in bondage. Why? Why? When Jesus made it plain that the Law is summed up in love. He said to love God with all your heart, soul and spirit, then to love your neighbor as yourself, and against that there is no law. That's the very love that was shed on Calvary.

Don't you get it? If you truly love, God's love, love that can only come from being filled with the gift of the Holy Spirit, the agape love, then you can't offend even the Law, and that love will bring you to your expected end. It's the lack of that agape love that is keeping you from your deliverance, from your blessings, from your inheritance in Christ.

Our Father is not holding back anything from His children because He said no good thing would He withhold from you. He said He has already blessed us with all spiritual blessing. It's already done, and it's waiting for us to come and get it.

I conclude this book by speaking to ALL of those women and even the men, for our Father has no respect of persons, you who are reading these words. God said, Today when you hear my voice harden not your heart. He is calling you out of darkness into the marvelous light. I pray your eyes of understanding be enlightened that you may know what is the hope of His calling, and what is the riches of His glory of His inheritance in you, the saints. I pray God stir up the gifts inside you that you bring forth fruit ripe for His kingdom knowing that the work He started in you He will bring to completion.

Receive this word, receive His word as spoken by the greatest Prophet ever, our Lord and Savior, Jesus Christ who now sits on the right hand of the Father making intercession for us all. Know that He has given us all power to defeat satan, and that He will keep you in perfect peace if you keep your mind stayed on Him.

Last but not least I offer you freedom. Freedom to love, freedom to live in this life. These are the steps:

1. Confess with your mouth and believe in your heart that Jesus Christ is Lord and He died for your sins. Romans 10:9
2. Ask for forgiveness of all your sins, even those 4 and 5 generations past, and forgive all those that have sinned against you. Matthew 6: 14,15
3. Ask for the gift of the Holy Ghost with evidence of speaking in other tongues. Acts 2:4
4. Study God's word, you open the word, the manual of life, daily and pray for revelation. 2 Timothy 2:15, Acts 17:11
5. Desire and pray for manifestation of the fruit of the spirit. Galatians 5: 22, 23
6. Seek your purpose, God's desire for you in this life and live in it. Romans 8:28, Ephesians 1: 11
7. Receive the blessings of God (everything) with thanksgiving. 1 Thessalonians 5:18

8. Truly have a relationship with our Father, His son, and the Holy Spirit. Become one in mind, body, soul and spirit. Ephesians 2: 18 - 22
9. Walk in your newness, a renewed mind every day. Romans 12: 1,2
10. Find yourself, let God lead you, to a Bible preaching, Bible teaching, Bible speaking and Bible living fellowship that believes in sowing into the kingdom. 2 Timothy 1: 10-13, 1 Corinthians 3: 8
11. Train your mouth to speak only good things (if you fill your spirit with the word of God you can only utter goodness). Psalms 103: 1, 5, Matthew 12: 34-37
12. Go and tell others what God has done for you. Go reconcile the World around you. 2 Corinthians 5: 17-19, Matthew 4:19

Don't be discouraged when you start your journey and the road seems all up hill. You see, it's the pain and struggles in your life that takes you to new levels, higher heights and deeper depths in Christ. The word says when Zion travailed; she brought forth in one day. Just like a pregnant woman, she knows it's time to give birth when the pain starts and it becomes more than she can bear, but that too shall pass, for weeping may endure for a night, but joy certainly comes in the morning light. The blessings of God are more than we can ask or think. He created this world for us and everything thing in it belongs to us, we must be about our Father's business so we can reap the harvest He has set aside for you and me.

Be blessed, I love you with an agape love. See you in the kingdom.

De Colores,

Cynthia

WORKS CITED

Abraham, Ken. Armed and Dangerous. Barbour Books, Ohio, 1991.

Brown, Rebecca and Daniel Yoder. Unbroken Curses. Whitaker House, PA, 1995.

Comparative Parallel Study Bible. Zondervan Pub. House, Michigan, 1984.

Copeland, Kenneth. You Are The Prophet of Your Own Life (tape series). Kenneth Copeland Ministries. Ft. Worth, TX.

Jakes, T.D. Sacred Love Songs (CD).

Jakes, T.D. The Lady, Her Lover and Her Lord. G. P. Putnam and Sons, New York, 1998.

Kindred, Jomaro F. <u>Seven.</u> A Poem.

Long, Eddie. The Church, Living Without Love (tape series). New Birth Ministries, Atlanta, GA.

Montgomery, Ed. Heaven In Your Heart Video Series, TX.

Morton, Paul. The Life Video Series.

Munroe, Myles. Single, Married, Separated and Life After Divorce. Destiny Image, Pub. Inc., PA 1992.

Strong, James. Strong Exhaustive Concordance. World Bible Pub. Inc., N.J. 1993.

Vanzant, Iyanla. One Day My Soul Just Opened Up. Fireside, New York, 1998.

Wills, Romuald. How to Find A Good Man. E.R.L. Publishing, Wash D.C., 1998.

ABOUT THE AUTHOR

Cynthia A. Williams is a born again, sanctified, Holy Ghost filled and fire baptized woman of God, who has been through. She was born and raised in the Tidewater area of Virginia, where Christ took her life in 1978.

Cynthia is an ordained minister of the word of God. She accepted her call to the ministry as an evangelist, later to have God call her to the Office of a Prophet. She flows in all the gifts of the spirit. God has birthed studies and books in her spirit. She has authored a commentary entitled "Marriage: Not Just A Simple "I Do." A commentary that ministers the truth about marriage, the covenant relationship of God.

Cynthia is the mother of four children, and four grandchildren. She just recently came together with her husband, her Adam, Chosen too. She is in the process of retiring from the United States Army. She has a degree from the University of Maryland and is going to pursue her call in the Ministry and her call to be a midwife, spiritually and naturally. She will be pursuing her ministry of the unborn, and a ministry "Free-Will Fellowship Ministries" in Virginia and via e-mail.

Cynthia answered the call from God. She is Chosen and a front line soldier in the Army of the Lord.

If you would like to contact the Author or order copies of the book, contact via e-mail at **cmillersmith@hotmail.com**,
Or go to your local bookstores and ask at the counter.

Any other they may obtain the book, such as Amazon.com.

Printed in the United States
5125